MAXIMUM FRIENDSHIP

JEFF &
RAMONA
TUCKER

Maximum FRIENDSHIP

**Devotions
for Students**

**Harold Shaw Publishers
Wheaton, Illinois**

For Albert and Josie Cramer,
who lovingly give us the best gift of all—their friendship.

A special thanks to
Evangeline and Brian, who've shown us that family can be best friends;
Jack, Corinne, and Charlene for their creative brainstorming;
and the HFC youth group for their good-natured role in being guinea
pigs for this book!

ISBN 0-87788-583-4

Cover and interior design by David LaPlaca
Cover photo credits: Jamie Marcial/SuperStock and Arthur Tilley/FPG International

Library of Congress Cataloging-in-Publication Data

Tucker, Jeff, 1960-
    Maximum friendship : devotions for students / Jeff and Ramona Tucker.
      p. cm.
    Rev. ed. of: No artificial flavors.
    ISBN 0-87788-583-4
    1. Teenagers—Prayer-books and devotions—English. 2. Friendship—Religious aspects—Christianity. I. Tucker, Ramona, 1962- . II. Tucker, Jeff, 1960- No artificial flavors. III. Title.
    BV4850.T825 1999
    241'.6762—dc21   98-54291

04 03 02 01 00 99

10 9 8 7 6 5 4 3 2 1

About the Authors

Jeff and Ramona Tucker have over thirty years of combined ministry experience with junior high and high school students. Jeff is a plant superintendent at a manufacturing facility and Ramona is Editor of *Today's Christian Woman* and Executive Editor of *Virtue.* They live in the Chicago area.

Contents

Week Four: Cliques & Clones Will Break My Bones

Week Five: A Walk in Your Shoes

Week Six: Nasty Little Papercuts

Week Seven: Buddies No Matter What

Preface
Check It Out!

When we asked the teens in our youth group to write down the three things that were most important to them, two tied for the #1 place: *Friends* and *Family*. *School or peer pressure,* which also has to do with friendship, took third!

Being a teen isn't easy—we know. You're faced with more concerns than ever before: peer pressure, self-esteem, romance, family problems, questions about whether God is really there or not. Maybe you're confused about who you are and just how you fit into this crazy, topsy-turvy world. Or perhaps you're lonely. You might have lots of "friends," but you still feel like you're in a locker all by yourself, and someone slammed the door.

Together we'll look at different types of friendships to discover tips for making the good ones last and for breaking off the not-so-good ones. And as we share the stories of the kids in this book, you'll find help for areas you're struggling in. Things like how to handle annoying siblings and snobbish cliques; how to forgive—and forget—friends when they drop you on the floor; how to solve sticky conflicts. We'll even look at the importance of guy/girl friendships and what's different about boy friends and boyfriends.

In these pages, you'll find space to write in, friendly suggestions for activities, and things to think or pray about during the rest of the day. Nothing would make us happier than to see this book well-worn and stained with your scribbles, thoughts, and discoveries.

But overall, we pray that you'll discover—in this book and in the pages of Scripture—a Friend who's got all the #1 qualities you could ever want or need. We'll let you fill in the name!

Week One
More or Less?

DAY ONE
Friendship Power

Tina was exasperated. She and Chris were at it again. She felt like throwing him and all his stubborn ideas right out the window. Friends were supposed to stick together, right? And think and act like twins?

Tina and Chris had been good friends for two years; they'd been drawn together like magnets. But lately she and Chris always rubbed each other the wrong way. Tina's family was conservative— She couldn't listen to anything but the mellowest Christian music and her curfew was at ten every night, even weekends.

Chris was almost exactly her opposite. His CD collection was mostly Christian rock, and his parents didn't even set a curfew. They said they trusted him to make his own wise decisions. Tina and Chris were always knocking heads over that one, wondering, "So who's right anyway?" They disagreed on a lot of other issues too.

Do Opposites Really Attract?
Friendship isn't automatic. You don't just push a button on a machine and ka-chink!—out falls a perfect, made-to-order friend. Actually, that would be pretty boring. You don't need a duplicate copy of yourself as a friend—it would be like staring at yourself every day.

Friendship doesn't always mean agreeing and being clones of each other. Differences can be good. They make us think and help us grow as persons. And they make us stronger persons because we have to make our own decisions. Good friends learn to compromise and to give each other freedom to be who they are. They are dedicated to each other and to learning how to make their relationship work. Good friends let each other be unique, and they challenge each other to become the absolute best they can be.

Unlikely People

Some of the most unlikely people in the Bible were friends. Take Moses and Aaron for example. Moses was a terrific organizer; God needed his talent when the Israelites were wandering in the desert. But Moses had a problem. He couldn't speak well—he'd get so nervous he'd stumble and stutter over his words. He needed his brother Aaron who was a great speaker, but tended to go off the deep end when Moses wasn't around. (When Moses trekked up the mountain to get the Ten Commandments, Aaron allowed the people to stumble in a major way—they built a golden calf to worship instead of God.)

Together Moses and Aaron were unstoppable. And what's more, they were even real live brothers! That's a pretty good example of what working together can do.

Two other friends who worked together at a task were Elijah and Elisha. A poor guy, Elijah was always running around the country without a roof over his head. Elisha, on the other hand, had five oxen (in Bible times that meant he was a lot better off). Today it would be like Elijah having a junker of a car while Elisha had a red Porsche 930 Turbo.

Even though they were about as far apart in social position and money as you could get, they still became close friends. They realized that differences were necessary and normal, but that each one of them still had a special place in God's plan.

Paul explained it in Romans 12:4-6:

> Just as each of us has one body with many members, and these members do not all have the same function, so in Christ we who are many form one body, and each member belongs to all the others. We have different gifts, according to the grace given us.

Like & Unlike
Evaluate your three closest friends. How are they like you?

_____

_____

Different from you?

_____

_____

Thank God today for giving you unique friends, and for giving you such a special place in his plans.

DAY TWO
Through Thick and Thin

Dad was on the warpath again. In fact, he seemed to be yelling even more than usual—which was most of the time.

Trish sighed. She and Dad could never agree on anything. Lately Trish had worked especially hard to keep her room clean and to help around the house, but Dad didn't seem to notice. Even when she did something extra, like washing Dad's car, Dad always found something wrong with it.

She felt like she couldn't even talk to her dad anymore. Whenever he came home, *if* he came home, he was drunk. And then when he got home, he'd have a drink in his hand within five minutes. She was tired of hearing her parents fight. They even fought when her friends came over. It was so embarrassing that she didn't ask anyone to come over anymore.

Except Candi. Candi was her always-there friend. They did everything together—worked at Burger King after school on Mondays and Wednesdays, sang in choir on Sundays, and went out together on weekends. They shared everything, down to diet Cokes and pocket change. When Trish's dad yelled, Candi didn't get embarrassed like Trish's other friends did. She just rolled her eyes and smiled that twinkly smile that made Trish feel immediately better. Candi understood and loved her just the same, alcoholic dad and all. She trusted Candi completely. Candi would do anything for her—she was that kind of friend.

A Loyal Friend
Candi was a loyal friend, both in time and heart. It didn't matter to

her one bit that Trish had a rough home life. She just took it in stride and went right on being a heart friend.

David and Jonathan had a loyal friendship like that. Even though they lived a long time ago, there are a lot of things we can learn from them. Jonathan was the son of a king, and David was only a shepherd boy. But that didn't stop them from being friends. Can you imagine? It's like the poorest kid in school with the rattiest clothes becoming the best friend of the richest, best-looking kid with all the name-brand clothes and a mansion of a house.

Brotherly Love

David and Jonathan had a special friendship. They grew to love each other like brothers, and they stuck together through thick and thin. You can read the story of their loyal friendship in 1 Samuel chapters 19 and 20. The Bible says this about faithful friends:

> Love each other with genuine affection, and take delight in honoring each other. Never be lazy in your work, but serve the Lord enthusiastically. Be glad for all God is planning for you. Be patient in trouble, and always be prayerful. When God's children are in need, be the one to help them out. *Romans 12:10-13, NLT*

Old Faithful

Do you have a special friend you feel like you can always count on? Why do you feel that way?

_____

_____

Are you a faithful, loyal friend? What can you do this week to become one?

_____

_____

Even When the Truth Hurts

I can't believe it! Tim muttered to himself as he plopped on his unmade bed. *Bruce is supposed to be a Christian.* Tim was ticked off. He had thought Bruce was a cool guy. He didn't wear the word SUPER CHRISTIAN plastered in capital letters across his chest or anything like that, but he was pretty cool, at least most of the time.

But lately things had changed. Tim's group of friends no longer seemed good enough for Bruce. And today at school, he'd heard that Bruce got drunk last night.

What good is all this stuff he told me about Christ anyway? It doesn't seem to make any difference to him now, Tim thought. He felt like phoning Bruce. After all, they *had* been good friends. And shouldn't friends be honest with each other?

He reached for the phone. But then wondered, *What if he gets mad when I ask him what he's up to? Or worse, what if he laughs at me?* Slamming down the phone, Tim dropped his chin into his hands. *I'm such a chicken.*

A Shot in the Arm

Bruce isn't the only one who needs a good buddy to turn him around. We all need it sometimes. Maybe we aren't doing something radical like getting drunk, but there are other things—like gossiping, having a bad attitude, or ignoring the new kid.

In Isaiah 38-39, we read a great story about two friends— Isaiah the prophet and Hezekiah the king. Hezekiah was a good guy, but he was also human. He made a big mistake. When the king of Babylon sent him a get-well present, it went to his head. He was so pleased that he showed the Babylonians (his country's enemies) where all his gold and silver and other treasures were. It was like showing a robber where you keep your money stashed.

Hezekiah didn't think past his own emotions to what he was doing to his kingdom and the people. When Isaiah heard about it, he marched directly to the king and confronted him, telling Hezekiah that because of what he had done, the Babylonians would invade the country and carry its people and treasures into captivity.

It Takes Guts

Isaiah was one gutsy dude. Even though the king could have anyone executed that he wanted to, Isaiah wasn't afraid. What meant more to Isaiah was keeping a covenant of honesty with his friend—even when his friend got off on the wrong track.

Most likely, none of your friends would have you executed, even if they got mad enough! But they might turn you off or go on doing what they are doing anyway. Still, God calls us to keep our friends accountable in their faith:

> Two are better than one . . . If one falls down, his friend can help him up. But pity the man who falls and has no one to help him up! Though one may be overpowered, two can defend themselves. A cord of three strands is not quickly broken. *Ecclesiastes 4:9-10, 12*

Good Medicine

When was the last time you told a friend the truth about something good in his or her life? Something bad?

_____

_____

Good friends hold each other accountable. Make a covenant with a friend to be honest with each other—even when the truth hurts.

DAY FOUR
Success—It's Up To You

Amy was a cute, petite blonde and was a junior at Glendale West in Ohio. The only problem was, she'd just transferred in from a school in Alabama.

Amy felt lost. Every day she dreaded going to school. The first day was the worst. Wandering down the hallways, she'd been looking for her English room. All of a sudden, a kid yelled at her, "Hey, frosh! You're not supposed to be in this hall. It's a SENIOR hall. Get lost!" She'd walked away with all the dignity she could muster.

Living in the North was very different. It felt like everything moved a lot faster and that kids weren't as friendly. Or maybe it just seemed that way because she didn't know anyone. She was too scared to open her mouth, because if she did, everyone would know she was different. She'd lived in Alabama all her life and she hadn't ever thought about "accents" until she moved to Ohio.

The first two months passed slowly. She still didn't have any friends. Between classes she walked alone, and she sat alone at lunch.

One Friday after school, she rushed home and up to her room. "I hate this place! Why did Mom have to move here anyway? No one likes me!" she yelled and threw herself on her bed. Then the tears came—a whole hour of them. Her eyes looked puffy the next day.

Making Your Own Success
How do you choose your friends? Sometimes it just happens, and you don't feel like you really *chose* anybody. Other times, maybe you're like Amy. You have a hard time reaching out beyond your-

self even to say "Hi y'all!" Maybe you feel insecure, and you wish that someone would just say hi and invite you out for a Coke.

Have you ever felt like Amy? If so, when?

_____

_____

How would you have responded to Amy if she had come to your school?

_____

_____

In order to have friends, you need to ask yourself: What kind of friend do I want to be? Friendship is more than *finding* the right person; it's *becoming* the right person.

Essentials

This week you've been thinking about some essential qualities of friendship—valuing people and their differences, loyalty, trust, honesty, commitment. Of course there are lots more, and we'll be discovering more in our next weeks together, but those qualities are just for starters.

If you focus on becoming loyal, trustworthy, and committed instead of groaning that you don't have friends, you might discover a few surprises. The Bible says this:

> Therefore, strengthen your feeble arms and weak knees. "Make level paths for your feet," so that the lame may not be disabled, but rather healed. *Hebrews 12:12-13*

It's up to you. You can either focus on your own loneliness and sink deeper into it, or you can look around and try to meet some of the needs that other people have. If you're concentrating on helping someone else, you won't have time to be self-conscious.

You'll find that you will start caring more about other people.

And guess what? They'll begin to realize what a good friend you are! Having a committed friend is the best!

Self-Check

Copy this verse and put it in your locker, your mirror, your car—some place where you will see it every day:

> If we love each other, God lives in us, and his love has been brought to full expression through us. . . . And God himself has commanded that we must love not only him but our Christian brothers and sisters, too. *1 John 4:12, 21,* NLT

Keep asking yourself, "What kind of friend do I want to be?" Remember—your success story is up to you.

DAY FIVE
Tough As Nails

I t was 3:00 P.M., and the school bell zinged through Terrin High. Randy grabbed his books and tore down the hallway, raced down the long steps and out to his beat-up Mustang. *All right! Freedom at last!* He cranked up his radio.

He was going to see Brian, his best football buddy. He'd agreed to bring his assignments over since Brian was stuck in bed. A week ago, Brian had been tackled and went down pretty hard. He broke his arm and his leg in five places. *What a bummer!* Randy thought. *I'd hate it if it were me.*

Then the months turned into winter. Going over to Brian's every day started to get a little old. *How far does this friendship thing go anyway?* Randy wondered, shivering and pulling up his collar. *You know, I need some time of my own. I didn't know it would take this much work or time. I'd really like to go out with the guys tonight and here I am, stuck going over to Brian's house again.*

A Committed Friend

Maybe you're like Randy. You're starting to feel like one of your friends is a real burden—too possessive of your time, or always down, or, like Brian, sick and out of commission. Sometimes you feel like blowing your friend off.

If anyone had a good reason to dump a friend, it was Jonathan. All the odds were against David. Jonathan's dad, King Saul, was really angry at David. Once Saul was so mad that he even threw a spear at David and tried to pin him to the wall!

When the Going Gets Tough

But that didn't stop Jonathan. When the going got tough, Jonathan got tougher. He helped David hide from Saul and devised a plan to find out if his dad really intended to kill David (see 1 Samuel 20). Jonathan risked the king's anger and got it. His dad even threw a spear at him!

Probably no one will ever throw an actual spear at you— spears went out with the Dark Ages and cannibals. But people might throw other spears at you. Things like, "How come you're hanging out with that guy? He's really weird." Or, "You're still *her* friend? Well, then, you can't be *my* friend." Then you have to decide if you will be a committed friend no matter what.

The Bible says this about a committed friend:

> There are "friends" who destroy each other, but a real friend sticks closer than a brother. *Proverbs 18:24, NLT*

Paraphrased, this verse means "indiscriminately chosen friends may bring trouble, but a genuine friend sticks with you through thick and thin" (*Ryrie New American Study Bible*). A genuine friend—like David, like Jonathan.

Sticking Together

What does being a committed friend mean to you?

_____

_____

Choose one friend to pray for this week. Pray that God will help you put your ideas about commitment into action.

Week Two
School Snapshots

DAY ONE
Shy Shari

It was the first day of Shari's sophomore year. She walked down the beige hallways, glancing to the left and then to the right. Her locker was here somewhere.

Where is #292? she wondered. She found #250 and #280, and then she saw them—the 290s. They were surrounded by a whole bunch of laughing guys and girls.

Shari's heart sank. Her head drooped as she hid behind her new notebook and oozed past her locker. She rounded the corner and pretended to take a long drink from the water fountain, anything to kill time. When she walked back to her locker, no one was there. Relieved, she opened the door and slid in her jacket.

What's my problem anyway? she muttered, ticked off at herself.

Then the bell rang. Oh no! She was late for class—and what was worse, on the very first day! Now she'd have to walk in and find her seat in front of everybody. Shari felt like crawling in her locker and shutting the door—permanently.

Totally Average
Maybe you're like Shari. You get so nervous when someone talks to you that you slam your thumb in your locker or drop your books (on their feet of course!). Or you don't feel you're good enough to be noticed because you're not good-looking, talented, or above average in anything.

Looking Beyond the Mirror
Ugh. How often have *you* looked in the mirror in the morning and

winced? You check out your hair, groan, and decide it's going to be a bad hair day. Or maybe you feel like you're ugly because you have truckloads of pimples, and you just don't want to be noticed until the Clearasil has done its job. You decide you may as well just give up and wear a paper bag over your head the rest of your life.

But God says that what you see on the outside is not what's most important in the long run (check 1 Samuel 16:7 for why). Yes, other people may look at your outside first, so you should be aware that others may judge you on your looks alone. But remember that God sees what's *inside.* Are you concentrating on your inside (your thoughts, emotions, attitudes) as much as on your outside?

Plucking Up Courage

After the Israelites wandered in the desert for forty years, Moses died. God appointed Joshua as the new leader and told him:

> As I was with Moses, so I will be with you; I will never leave you nor forsake you . . . Be strong and courageous. Do not be terrified; do not be discouraged, for the LORD your God will be with you wherever you go. *Joshua 1:5, 9*

If God could do that for Joshua, who was in charge of thousands of people, he can do it for you, too! The next time you feel like dog-food (and maybe think you look like it), reread that verse.

Do you know any people like Shy Shari? (Maybe it's you.) Make some notes about what you could say to him or her this week.

_____

_____

Write out the verse above so you can carry it with you. Or use it to encourage a friend!

DAY TWO
Toss-Aside Tim

Hey Tim!" Jerry's voice boomed across the parking lot. "How was your date with Colleen last night?"

"Terrific!" Tim grinned, showing perfect white teeth. "She's a great girl." As he slicked his brown hair back, it fell perfectly back into place.

All the girls thought Tim was Hunk-of-the-Year. Always perfectly dressed in the right clothes, he was the biggest stud of Fremont High. And he knew it.

"Are you going out with her again?" Jerry asked.

"Naw. She's O.K. and everything, but really not my type." And Tim went on to explain for five minutes why she wasn't.

Tim treated everyone alike—it didn't matter whether they were guys or girls. He was a be-a-friend-once-and-then-toss-aside guy. Why shouldn't he? Tim figured he had his pick of anyone he wanted to be friends with. They were all at his feet, begging to be his friend because he was such a cool guy and all.

Jerry shook his head. He just couldn't understand Tim.

Straight to the Head

Perfect Tim. He was a popular guy. The only problem was he let it go straight to his head. Ever heard the saying, "His head's so fat he couldn't get it through the doorway?" Well, Tim's was so big it could have taken over the world—or at least his world, Fremont High.

Right now it's cool to be like Tim. But sooner or later, Tim's going to fall over his own feet and—*splat!* There goes the reputation. Suddenly he won't seem so handsome anymore. You can't toss people aside or treat them like objects for long. Soon they won't want to be around you.

Attitude Check

In Philippians 2:3-4, Paul says,

> Do nothing out of selfish ambition or vain conceit, but in humility consider others better than yourselves. Each of you should look not only to your own interests, but also to the interests of others.

Evaluate yourself honestly. How do you treat other kids at school?

_____

_____

Write down examples from specific situations that you'd like to change.

_____

_____

Ask God to help you treat others the way you would want to be treated.

DAY THREE
Merry Mary?

Good morning, Joy! Isn't it just be-e-eautiful today? I love spring, don't you?" Mary gushed as she came into Joy's room.

Joy groaned as she turned over in bed. Every morning it was the same scene. She felt like ducking back under her covers and hiding. Since Mary was also a junior and lived on her block, she had taken it upon herself to meet at Joy's house and walk with her to school every day.

This is disgusting! Go away! Joy exclaimed inside.

Mary bubbled, "I just couldn't wait to get up today so I could wear my new jeans to school. The girls are going to love them, don't you think?"

Joy propped open her blue eyes—just a corner though. Enough to see Mary perched on the edge of her bed, looking 110 percent awake and ready to go, as usual.

Joy sighed and dragged herself up in a fog while Mary chattered on happily. *She can't be this happy all the time! It's impossible!* Joy thought. Joy put on a semi-smile while she threw on her jeans and a rumpled t-shirt.

Bursting the Bubble

We all know someone like Merry Mary. Maybe it's the girl at school who is always so bubbly that you want to smash her because *nobody* could be that happy all the time. Or maybe it's the guy who's the clown of the class, who laughs even when the other kids give him a hard time.

Merry Mary may have always seemed happy on the outside, but

what was happening on the inside? What Joy didn't know was that Mary's parents were breaking up. Every night they fought. It echoed in Mary's brain. Scared they'd get a divorce and yet wanting the screaming to end, Mary felt caught—and guilty. She wondered if it were her fault.

The up-front happy stuff was just a big fake. Too embarrassed to tell anyone what was going on at home, Mary hid her problems.

Real People

No matter what people act like, you have to look beyond their words and actions to what they're *really* thinking and feeling. Maybe they need you to ask, "How are you *really* doing?" and to take time for them. They need you to show that you care about them and are interested in them personally. In Galatians, Paul encourages us to keep doing good for others:

> Let us not become weary in doing good, for at the proper time we will reap a harvest if we do not give up. Therefore, as we have opportunity, let us do good to all people, especially to those who belong to the family of believers. *Galatians 6:9-10*

If someone you know is happy, it doesn't always mean that they have personal problems. But be sensitive. You might be surprised what you find out when you keep your eyes and ears open.

The Great Pretenders

There are lots of reasons why people may try to pretend things are fine when they're really not. When have *you* worn a big smile when inside your were really in turmoil? Why? What could you do next time?

_____

_____

_____

How can you become the kind of person that others will confide in and not feel they have to pretend?

_____

_____

Ask Jesus to give you a new, special love for the Merry Marys in your life.

One-Track Ted

Ted was Mr. Average in just about everything. But he could be considered almost handsome—until he opened his mouth that is. Then he bored everyone to death.

Ted was at it again. Andrea could tell he was interested in her, and she sort of liked him. So she had invited him over to her house yesterday after school. He'd even offered to carry her books. She couldn't believe it! He was so-o-o nice.

Then he blew it. Big time. When they climbed Andrea's front porch steps, they'd run into her brother Brian. Both Brian and Ted were into cars. And not just into them—they breathed, ate, and slept cars. Talking about engines to them was like eating chocolate chip cookies to Andrea. They had spent two hours talking about turbo chargers and dual exhausts, and finally took off to see the car Brian was overhauling in the garage, leaving Andrea slumped and bored on the porch.

She hadn't even seen Ted the rest of the evening. He'd waved goodbye and yelled happily, "Hey, thanks for inviting me!"

Today, Ted was at her locker again. "Andrea, your brother is terrific! And he knows so much." Ted launched off into lingo about boosting his car's horsepower again. Andrea felt like screaming.

One-Track Minds

Everyone knows a one-focused guy or girl. Maybe like Ted, the car expert, he talks about cars every time one rolls by. When you try to switch the subject, he looks at you blankly like you don't exist. Maybe it's Lori, whose mind holds only visions of the nearest shopping mall. Or Bob, the Bible-banger, whose Bible is so big he can't even stuff it in his locker.

When these people are around, you probably feel like killing them (even if you're a good kid and the thought of murder would never enter your mind otherwise). They always seem to crank their mouths in gear, but rarely their ears.

Switching Tracks

What words do you think describe one-track people? Maybe selfish, insensitive. But have you ever thought that maybe they just don't know what else to talk about? They feel insecure, so they pick one subject that they know more about than anyone else. Or they could be genuinely interested in a certain subject and honestly don't know they're boring you to death.

But you know what? If you really choose to listen and actually show interest, you might learn something. Even better, they might realize they have a genuine friend in you and start listening to what *you* have to say. The Bible encourages us to put guts behind what we say and do: "Dear children, let us not love with words or tongue but with actions and in truth" (1 John 3:18).

How 'Bout You?

Are you like Ted? Wanting to talk only about the things you're interested in? Do you get bored easily? Make notes here about your last two conversations today. (If you can't remember them, maybe that's a clue about your listening powers!)

_____

_____

How can you show someone you're really listening to them? How can this be part of loving "with actions and in truth"?

_____

_____

This week, when someone is boring you, turn your ears on. You might learn something about them or even yourself! Ask God to make you a more sensitive listener.

DAY FIVE
Can't-Make-Up-My-Mind Carol

Hey, Carol! Are you going to Shelly's party Friday?" wheezed Jackie, a little out of breath from her dash down the school halls. Jackie never walked; she always took off like she'd seen the biggest, hairiest spider that ever crawled.

"Everybody's going! Susan, Andy, and . . ." Jackie chattered on. Everyone who was *anyone* she meant. There were about ten kids in Carol's and Jackie's group who hung out together.

"Are you going, Jack?" Carol asked quietly.

"You bet! It's gonna be great."

"Well, if you're going, I guess I'll go," Carol said slowly.

"Great! See you later!" Jackie called and tore down the hall.

Carol bumped into Cyndi on the way to her bicycle. "Want to grab a Coke, Carol?" Cyndi asked, flipping her blonde hair back. "I'm meeting the others there."

"I guess I'll go, if you're going," Carol hesitated.

Cyndi drawled, rather exasperatedly, "Well, come on, let's get going. We're already late."

All the girls knew Carol couldn't make up her mind about anything. Whether it was choosing a movie or where to eat (she couldn't even pick from the menu without seeing what her friends chose first!), or even what to wear. That was just Carol. It always had been and probably always would be. Her friends had gotten used to it.

Wishy-Washy People

How many people do you know who are like Carol? People who

can't make up their minds are usually insecure—they so want to be a part of a group that they're afraid of making a different decision than everyone else. Fitting into a particular group is more important than being who they really are.

Carol had a hard time standing up for anything. She was a major pushover, and everyone knew it. But there's more about Carol. The sad thing is, she can't even stand up for what she believes in. Things like dating standards and religion. Whether she acts like a Christian or not depends on whom she's with.

Stand-Up Power

The Bible says this about wishy-washy people: "A doubtful mind is as unsettled as a wave of the sea that is driven and tossed by the wind. People like that should not expect to receive anything from the Lord. They can't make up their minds. They waver back and forth in everything they do" (James 1:6-8, NLT). And Revelation 3:15-16: "I know your deeds, that you are neither cold nor hot; I wish you were either one or the other! So, because you are luke-warm—neither hot nor cold—I am about to spit you out of my mouth."

God wants us to learn to take a stand, whether it's easy or not. Making decisions is part of the growing-up process.

Firm Ground

Have you ever been wishy-washy on a decision? If so, when? What was the result?

_____

_____

What could you do the next time you're struggling with wishy-washiness?

_____

_____

If you have a hard time making up your mind on things, remember what Paul says in Philippians:

> And this is my prayer: that your love may abound more and more in knowledge and depth of insight, so that you may be able to discern what is best and may be pure and blameless until the day of Christ . . . then make my joy complete by being like-minded, having the same love, being one in spirit and purpose. *Philippians 1:9-10; 2:2*

Copy these verses into a notebook or post them on your bathroom mirror so you'll always have them when you need them. In your prayer time today, ask God to help you stand firm.

Week Three

Guys & Gals:
A Great Combo

DAY ONE
Friends & Veggies: They're Good for You

Finally it was done! Carmen was so relieved. Evan had been working on Carmen's stereo system for at least three hours. Some wires had shorted out, and, as always, Evan was available. *Mr. Handyman* he called himself and that's what he was. He could fix anything—cars, stereos, blowdryers, you name it. He even helped Carmen's parents fix their bathroom faucet when it constantly dripped.

"Evan, you're such a great guy. I can't believe I'm so lucky!" Carmen exclaimed.

"I know!" Evan grinned his cocky smirk and plopped back into the lambswool beanbag. Carmen could always count on him for a good laugh (or a good cry, whichever she needed).

Evan and Carmen had been good friends for over two years. He could always tell if she was upset about something and knew just how to draw her out. After all, who could resist that crazy, fun-loving, sensitive guy? He always put her in a better mood. Even Carmen's parents loved him because he was so comfortable, like an old pair of tennis shoes.

Carmen and Evan could talk about anything. It was cool how they could share things from different perspectives, without feeling threatened—or trying to impress each other—because they weren't dating. They were just solid-as-a-rock friends.

Top Teamwork
How many times have you heard, "Eat your vegetables. They're

good for you!" Since you were a toddler? Probably too many times to count. But it's true—veggies *are* good for you; they give your body some of the essential vitamins it needs to grow and be strong. Vitamins and your body make a dynamite team.

Friendships with the opposite sex can be wonderful and healthy, like eating veggies. Carmen's and Evan's is just one example. But all too often, it seems that the only guy/girl relationships are dating ones. Guys and girls could learn a lot from each other that would help in future relationships—things like how each sex acts, thinks, and reacts differently.

Research statistics show that one of the top qualities listed by couples with loving, lasting marriages is friendship. The couples knew each other as friends *before* they started dating. In some cases, they didn't even think of dating each other until several years later when it finally clicked.

Without the commitment of friends, you can be very lonely. Make it a goal to find kids of both sexes with whom you can be friends.

A Common Goal

The Bible gives a wonderful example of a man and woman who supported each other—Deborah and Barak. In fact, they were so necessary to each other that Barak wouldn't go into battle without Deborah (you can read their story in the book of Judges, chapters 4–5). Imagine that! And especially in a time when women's roles were vastly different than they are today.

Proverbs 27:17 says:

As iron sharpens iron,
A friend sharpens a friend. (*NLT*)

And Ecclesiastes 4:9 says,

Two are better than one,
Because they have a good return for their work.

Friends are like that—they make us into better people, stretch our minds, and encourage our gifts.

One-a-Day Vitamins

Good friends of the opposite sex are like vitamins—necessary to your health. If you are a guy, do you have girl friends or girlfriends? If you are a girl, do you have boy friends or boyfriends? What's the difference?

_____

_____

How do you treat the opposite sex? Is there someone of the opposite sex you'd like to be closer friends with (not as a date!)?

_____

_____

If you're lonely, ask Jesus to send you friends—of both sexes.

DAY TWO
We're Just Friends—Honest

You and Marie are such a cute couple," Stephanie whispered. Dave grimaced. Stephanie *would* have to pipe up during his favorite part of the movie. She was just like that. He hoped Marie didn't hear her.

Everyone thought he and Marie were a hot item—except him and Marie! They were very good friends, but *just friends.* Why couldn't anyone understand that? They'd been friends for seven years, even at the age when guys and girls weren't supposed to like being friends. They drove together to band practice and football games in Dave's rattly Chevy and ate lunch together.

They loved each other—as friends. And they felt so comfortable together—except when people kept nagging them.

Dave groaned. *Why did everyone make such a big deal out of him and Marie?* It was downright embarrassing.

"Steph, we're not a couple. We're just friends," Dave responded.

"Yeah, sure. So how come you're always together?" Stephanie demanded.

No one will ever understand. Dave sighed. *Only Marie and me.* He gave up trying to explain to Steph and just pointed out, "You're missing the best part of the movie!" Then he leaned back in his chair, exasperated.

Missing the Boat
A lot of guys and girls have great relationships just as friends—like Dave and Marie. Maybe you do. And you've been put in a position very much like them, and you hate it. You feel like it's ruining your

friendship. You want to clobber the people who keep bugging you because they are totally missing the boat on this one.

What's Underneath

Have you ever wondered why some kids tease others, or make wrong assumptions? Maybe they're just downright rotten kids, and they love to give you a hard time. Or maybe it's because, deep down, they know they don't have good friends, and they're jealous. Or maybe they've never known or experienced a close friendship with a member of the opposite sex and can't understand. They could be feeling lonely, wishing they had a friend like yours.

Understanding Motives

Maybe you're in the position of Dave and Marie. Or maybe you relate more to Stephanie. Whichever position fits, put yourself in the other person's shoes. Make a list of how they could be feeling here:

_____

_____

The Bible says a lot about enduring things with patience—even pesky people like Stephanie:

> Our great desire is that you will keep right on loving others as long as life lasts, in order to make certain that what you hope for will come true. Then . . . you will follow the example of those who are going to inherit God's promises because of their faith and patience. . . . This confidence is like a strong and trustworthy anchor for our souls. *Hebrews 6:11-12, 19, NLT*

No matter where you are, you can always escape—to God. He gives us a wall of refuge that no one can penetrate. Take time to thank him for that today. Ask him to remind you of those verses the next time you get upset with pesky people.

DAY THREE
Lovin' Feelings

Remember Evan and Carmen from Day One? Well, there's more to their story. As Evan and Carmen spent more time together, Carmen started realizing that Evan was really more than a friend for her.

I've got incredibly warm feelings every time he's around, Carmen thought. *But I'm so scared. What if he doesn't feel the same way?*

They had both talked a lot about friendship the last year and how neither one of them really wanted to date anyone. They were just happy with who they were and neither wanted to get involved in a serious relationship—with anyone.

I don't want to lose his friendship, Carmen moaned, burying her face in her pillow. *What if I'm way off? Maybe he'll dump me.*

Carmen knew Evan enough to know that he didn't like leechy girls. When girls got too close, Evan backed off.

What a mess! Carmen sighed. She hoped Evan wouldn't come over tonight. She didn't want to see him until she had her head straightened out again.

What Do I Do Now?
Carmen was in a mess. And she'd put herself there. What she didn't know was that Evan felt the same way. And he was as scared as she was—he didn't want to lose a friend either. What if it didn't work out? Could they go back to being just friends? Or would their relationship be ruined forever? It was a big gamble.

What's Love Anyway?

How many times do you hear someone say, "I think I'm in love!!"?
Probably at least three times a day at school. Everyone has crushes
and what others might call "puppy love." But real love? Is there
such a thing? Here's what the Bible says about it:

> Love is patient, love is kind. It does not envy, it does not boast,
> it is not proud. It is not rude, it is not self-seeking, it is not
> easily angered, it keeps no record of wrongs. Love does not
> delight in evil but rejoices with the truth. It always protects,
> always trusts, always hopes, always perseveres. Love never
> fails. *1 Corinthians 13:4-8*

Doublecheck

If you think you're in love, doublecheck how you feel with the
Scripture passage above. Do you really love that particular person,
or are you in love with "being in love?" Do you sincerely love *that*
particular person, or do you just want *a* person? Be honest as you
jot down your thoughts.

_____

_____

What are the pros and cons of being friends first, rather than dating?

_____

_____

If you're "in love," talk to a trusted adult (a parent, teacher, youth
leader) about how you feel. Get their perspective to make sure your
love stacks up against the words of 1 Corinthians 13.

DAY FOUR
I Only Have Eyes for You

Rick and Robin had dated for about six months. At first, they just went out together on Saturday nights for pizza. But within the first month, it had begun to be every night. Then it got heavy. Robin just died if she didn't see Rick before school, at lunch, after school, and in the evening. She even left mushy love notes in his locker between classes.

Char was worried. This was getting pretty serious. She liked Rick a lot, and Robin was her best friend, but she felt left out. Robin and Rick were exclusive.

One Friday night when she and Robin were leaving together for a movie, Rick called. She heard Robin say, "No, I'm not doing anything. Be right over." As Char trudged home through the snow, she felt left in the cold once again. And that wasn't the only time. It became a ritual. She'd ask Robin to do something, then Rick would call up.

Char wanted to toss Robin right into the trash.

Exclusiveness

Char wasn't the only one who wanted to give up on Robin and Rick. Rick's guy friends felt the same way. But they weren't as persistent as Char. They just gave up and wrote him off.

Getting the brush off because "I'm-too-starry-eyed-over-my-boyfriend" hurts way down deep. But have you ever thought of something else? Not only does it hurt *you*, it also hurts *them*.

Does every couple who dates stay together through all of high school? Or all of life? Certainly not. Robin was already on her third "serious" boyfriend, and she was only a sophomore!

If a couple who's dating breaks up, what happens? They really need their friends. But if they've constantly dumped their friends to spend time with their boyfriend/girlfriend, they could be in big trouble. People may not want to be around them anymore.

The Choice Is Ours

Only two people—Adam and Eve—could afford to be exclusive. They were the first created humans on earth, and they had the whole garden to themselves. But we don't. We're constantly surrounded by people who need us and our friendship. Today we can't be an Adam or an Eve. Our world is not like that. (And besides, you'd be pretty embarrassed meeting your date dressed only in fig leaves!)

Banana Splits or Skins?

If you're interested in another guy or girl, how do you treat your friends around your "flame"? Do you treat them as special and wonderful—like going out for banana splits—or do you treat them like Robin treated Char—like old banana skins? Jesus talked about the way that we should treat others:

> So in everything, do to others what you would have them do to you, for this sums up the Law and the Prophets. *Matthew 7:12*

If you're dating someone now, write down how you're treating your other friends. If you aren't dating anyone at this time, write down how you feel around one of your friends who is dating.

_____

_____

Are you pleased with your actions? Ask God to make you more aware of your friends' feelings.

DAY FIVE
How Close Is Too Close?

Jenny and Alan had met in sixth grade at their church. But it wasn't until their junior year of high school that they'd really noticed each other. Alan thought Jenny was one of the cutest girls he'd ever seen, so he asked her out. On their first date, they discovered they both loved carnivals and rollercoasters.

They had such a blast together that they decided to go out again—on Friday. Jenny would never forget that night—she couldn't believe a kiss could turn you to marshmallow inside. So they kissed again. And again. And then suddenly they were rolling around on Alan's couch (his parents were gone for the evening), and clothes were everywhere.

It had happened so fast. Jenny woke up the next morning, her head whirling. *How could I let that happen? But it felt so good I didn't want to stop.* Jenny felt incredibly guilty. She wondered how Alan felt. After all, they were both Christians and really involved in their youth group. Jenny hoped it wouldn't ruin their friendship, but somehow she felt it already had.

No Fooling
Fooling around has consequences. Jenny was right. It had ruined a friendship that was just beginning to flourish. Alan steered clear of her at youth group for over five months, and then he started to date someone else. They had both lost their trust and respect for each other.

We've all heard the consequences of sex before marriage—the possibility of getting AIDS, herpes, and related diseases, or getting pregnant. Sure, that's enough to scare us, but is it enough to stop us from getting sexually involved outside of marriage?

God's Plan

In 1 Corinthians 6:18-20, God commands us to keep our bodies holy and pure:

> Run away from sexual sin! No other sin so clearly affects the body as this one does. For sexual immorality is a sin against your own body. Or don't you know that your body is the temple of the Holy Spirit, who lives in you and was given to you by God? You do not belong to yourself, for God bought you with a hight price. So you must honor God with your body. *(NLT)*

God doesn't tell us that because he wants to be a cosmic killjoy. He does it because he loves us and wants to protect us. For he knows that when our bodies get involved, so do our minds. It's much harder to break off a relationship that isn't a good thing if you've been sexually involved with each other. Why? Because no matter what happens in the relationship (and many times relationships based on sex fall apart within a few months because the guy and girl can't communicate except through sex), a part of you will still stay with that guy or girl.

God's plan is for only a husband and wife to be "in bed" together. If you've had premarital sex with one or more girls or guys, you'll be haunted by sexual ghosts when you make love with your spouse. Given the choice, wouldn't you pick a committed-for-a-lifetime love over a series of short flings?

There's Hope

If you have been involved in premarital sex, don't despair. There's hope for you. If you're truly sorry for what you have done, then ask God for his forgiveness. He gives it with open arms: "If we confess our sins, he is faithful and just and will forgive us our sins and purify us from all unrighteousness" (1 John 1:9).

But you must also take action. If you're still having sex, take steps so that it doesn't happen again. Avoid being alone with the other person—especially in places where it'd be easy to slip into old patterns—or break totally away from the person. (Most couples discover that without the sex, they don't have much in common anymore.)

Whether you're in this situation right now or not, you could be in the near future. Write down your guidelines for dating here. You might even ask a good Christian friend to hold you accountable and help you follow your guidelines. Then stick to them no matter what.

_____

_____

If your friends who've had sex are telling you how great it is, or are teasing you about being a virgin, remember one very important thing: You can become like them any day, but they can *never* again be like you. If you or a friend are in this situation now, claim the power of Christ in 1 Corinthians 10:13:

> No temptation has seized you except what is common to man. And God is faithful; he will not let you be tempted beyond what you can bear. But when you are tempted, he will also provide a way out so that you can stand up under it.

If you're really struggling to do the right thing—to stay a virgin or stop having sex with your boyfriend or girlfriend—talk to a trusted adult (teacher, parent, or youth leader). They can help you take steps and will provide a strong support for you along the way.

Week Four
Cliques & Clones Will Break My bones

DAY ONE
Who Put These Price Tags On Anyway?

Julius slammed the padlock on his athletic locker. *I'm such a clod!* he thought. *How come I have to be so uncoordinated?* He picked at the worn leather on his football. He felt pretty lucky just to make it on the junior varsity team this year.

Julius felt like he was constantly messing up. And that everyone saw him trip over his size 13 feet at least once a day. Like a giant Labrador, he galloped through the school halls. He never could get his arms and legs to go in the same direction at the same time. And besides that, he had braces—a full set of gleaming metal, that knocked your eyeballs out when he smiled.

I wish I were like Ron. He always has it together—and he's even got muscles in all the right places! Julius kicked his locker for the third time that day.

"I Wish" Syndrome

Have you ever wished you looked like someone else? Or even *were* someone else? Maybe you've battled with being chunky your whole life—you look at a Hershey's candy bar and it melts right onto your hips—or, even worse, onto your face. Maybe you're a senior, but you only weigh 89 pounds. The only position you could play on the football team is the football. Or maybe your parents are divorced, and you wish you had perfect parents like your friends.

One-of-a-Kind

There are lots of reasons why you could wish you were someone else. But you know what? God created you uniquely you.

> Before I formed you in the womb I knew you,
> before you were born I set you apart. *Jeremiah 1:5*

God knew you even while you were being created! And he made you as you are—a redhead, an athlete, a good cook, whatever. He gave you naturally wavy or straight-as-a-stick hair. And by putting together millions of variations, he made you—and there's no one else exactly like you in the whole world!

God values your uniqueness. And because he has created you as you are, he expects you to use what he's given you. Maybe you aren't the greatest athlete in the world, but you can bake up a storm. Then bake brownies for someone who is down. Maybe you're not a mechanical genius on cars like your buddy, but you are great with math. Then tutor someone who's really struggling.

Don't slip into the common trap of determining your self-worth by outward things like grades or good looks. We're created in the image of God (see Ephesians 2:10)—so we already have worth! Like Julius, we need to take our eyes off ourselves, off "How do I look? How am I doing?" and put them on helping someone else.

Through Your Own Eyes

Have you wished to be someone else? Who, and why?

_____

_____

List the things you're good at.

_____

_____

_____

How can you use these unique talents you've just listed to help others?

_____

_____

The next time you wish you were someone else, refer back to your list. Thank God that he made you uniquely you!

DAY TWO
Steamy Situations

Maria scooted over toward the car window. She couldn't believe she'd let herself get into this. Here she was—at Romantic Ridge—with José.

Maria had been so excited when José asked her out on Friday night for a double date with Marcy and Greg. The movie had been fun. But then, just as they were on their way to Pizza Hut, Marcy had said, "Hey, guys, let's make a detour for a few minutes."

When Maria agreed to the detour, she didn't know they'd end up at Romantic Ridge. But here they were. Marcy and Greg were kissing up a storm in the front seat. Maria felt pretty uncomfortable sitting in the back seat. She hoped no one would recognize her.

Firm Like a Rock
If you were Maria, what would you do? Crawl under the car seat? Maria is in a hard position. She doesn't want to be "chicken," but she knows that people who park at Romantic Ridge don't have good reputations either. She doesn't want to be like them.

Peer pressure is tough. You face it every day. And even though it's common, it doesn't make it easier. You have to make decisions about what kind of clothes you're going to wear, where you're going to go with your friends, what crowd you're going to hang around with, and what kind of a date you want to be.

You're Not the Only One
You're not the only one who had to face tough decisions about dating practices. Joseph did too. He was in his twenties, at the height

of his sexual drive, when Potiphar's wife, an older lady, went after him. Her persuasion wasn't subtle either: basically she tried to drag him into her bed (Genesis 39:12). And the poor guy had to flee from her without his coat!

Maybe someone isn't trying to "make out" or "go all the way" with you, but you still have hard choices to make about all kinds of temptation—sexual or otherwise. Joseph knew what to do with temptation. He ran away from it, because he knew God wouldn't be pleased if he gave in.

When the Pressure's On

James encourages us to take a stand when things are tough:

> Dear brothers and sisters, whenever trouble comes your way, let it be an opportunity for joy. For when your faith is tested, your endurance has a chance to grow. So let it grow, for when your endurance is fully developed, you will be strong in character and ready for anything. . . . God blesses the people who patiently endure testing. Afterward they will receive the crown of life that God has promised to those who love him. *James 1:2-4, 12,* NLT

Even though the consequences of obeying God weren't easy (Joseph was thrown in prison because he was falsely accused of attempted rape), God honored him. Later he became one of the head honchos over the land of Egypt and had all the wealth and power he ever could have imagined! God will also honor you for standing up for him—maybe not with riches or power, but through a good reputation, among other things.

When have you faced a peer-pressure decision? What did you do then? What would you do now?

_____

_____

God can give you the power to resist any temptation. Ask him for it.

DAY THREE
Who's Your Hero?

Sonya and J.D. bounced up and down in their seats. They couldn't wait for the concert to start. After saving up for the tickets, they knew it'd be worth it. And they'd even talked Mom and Dad into letting them go—a major miracle.

It was almost eight o'clock. Soon she'd come on. They couldn't believe they were actually going to see her after listening to her CDs for two years. And this year she'd been in the top ten almost every week.

But after the concert, J.D.'s and Sonya's steps slowed as they walked home. They were both disappointed—maybe she wasn't all they'd built her up to be. The concert was pretty good, but not what they expected. She only sang two of her hit songs, and the rest must have been old stuff they didn't know.

Hero Worship
All of us have heroes. When we were kids, it might have been our father or mother, or the ice cream man who drove the truck with the jingly bells. Maybe now it's a rock or movie star. It could be your favorite macho lawyer on TV or the girl on the commercials with the perfect body.

But whoever your hero is, you need to stand that person up next to this passage of Scripture:

> Be imitators of God, therefore, as dearly loved children and live a life of love. . . . There must not be even a hint of sexual immorality, or of any kind of impurity, or of greed. . . . Nor

should there be obscenity, foolish talk or coarse joking, which are out of place, but rather thanksgiving. . . . For you were once darkness, but now you are light in the Lord. . . . Be very careful, then, how you live—not as unwise but as wise, making the most of every opportunity, because the days are evil. *Ephesians 5:1-4, 8, 15-16*

Not All They're Cracked Up to Be

Human heroes usually aren't all we think they are. And sometimes we're disappointed—like J.D. and Sonya were. When that happens, the hero takes a rather nasty fall off your pedestal. Usually it's pretty hard for him to get back on. Even if he does manage it, now you see the cracks where you had to glue him back together.

Maybe this has happened in your own family. You've found out that Dad—whom you thought was perfect—has been having an affair. Or Mom, the always happy and stable lady, had to take off work for a month because of mental depression. Or maybe you discovered that your older brother whom you adore is gay. You're all confused.

There is only one real hero. This hero never falls off his pedestal because he can't sin—it's not a part of his nature. He is always perfect, something hard for us to imagine. Who's the real hero? Jesus Christ, the only one who will never fail or disappoint us. And even better, he's approachable—at any time, at all times. You don't even have to buy tickets to see him!

On the Pedestal

List two people who influence your decisions the most. In light of God's standards in Ephesians 5, are they a positive or negative influence on you? Give specifics.

_____

_____

Ask God to give you his kind of wisdom about whom you put on your pedestal.

DAY FOUR
The Lone Ranger

Jack the Jock strutted down the hall of Lincoln High. His classmates turned from their chatter to watch him. Last night, as usual, he had wowed them all at the soccer game by scoring a hat-trick (three goals) in a tough game against Westmont. The guy was incredible—*Super Stuff* they called him. He was good at anything and everything athletic and was even captain of the varsity baseball team (as a junior!).

He was such a together guy. He did everything well, and what's more, he did it by himself. His grades topped the chart. And because he was such an awesome guy, the other kids didn't even get mad when he wrecked the grading curve.

But somehow, Jack steered clear of his classmates. It wasn't that Jack was mean or sulky or anything like that, he just didn't hang around with them. They couldn't figure out why. Then after awhile, they convinced themselves, "Well, he doesn't need us anyway. He's got everything he needs."

Meanwhile, Jack padded down the halls to class alone.

On the Outside
On the outside, Jack seemed totally independent. But what was he like on the inside?

What nobody knew was that Jack stayed aloof on purpose. He wanted friends, but he was scared for anyone to get to know him too well. Because his dad had divorced his mom, he felt he had to be the man of the house now. Two years after the divorce, his mom still acted like a basket case and threatened to kill herself when she got depressed. And what's worse, both of his parents were supposed to be Christians.

At the Heart

All of us know someone who's a loner. Usually we label them in categories: "She's a band fag"; "He's a nerd"; "She's so stuck up"; "He's a jock"; because then we can box them up neatly. It's easy to attach stereotypes to someone because of their age, social rank, or sex. How many times have you heard generalizations like: "All teenagers are irresponsible!" "Dumb blonde!" "Teenage drivers!"? Jesus had some stern words for those who judge others:

> "Do not judge, or you too will be judged. For in the same way you judge others, you will be judged, and with the measure you use, it will be measured to you." *Matthew 7:1-2*

In other words, if you name-call and categorize other people, the same thing will happen to you.

In Their Shoes

Who's the lone ranger in your school? Put yourself in his or her place for a minute. How do you think that person really feels?

_____

_____

Write down one thing you can do for this person this week and then do it, knowing that God's smiling because of your actions. Ask a parent, youth leader, or close friend to keep you accountable.

_____

_____

DAY FIVE
The Right Kind of Nit-picky

Linda's mind churned. She was in a real pickle. Finally the "cool" kids had invited her to go out with them Friday night. But there was a big problem—they were going to a park that was way out in the country, a place known for wild parties.

She wanted to do something with them because they seemed like they had a lot of fun together. But still she was uncomfortable. She knew her parents wouldn't approve. So she told her friends no. Raising their eyebrows, they said, "Hey, babe, it's your loss."

But the next Monday she knew different. Shock waves skittered across the school. Everyone knew by noon hour about the terrible accident. Three of the kids who'd talked to her were dead. The driver had been drunk, and they'd found beer in the car.

The car I would have been riding in, Linda thought. Her stomach turned for the rest of the day.

Life Is a Cafeteria

Life is like going through a cafeteria line—we pick and choose the things that look good to us. One day of bad choices in food might not kill us (unless we get the stuff the cafeteria *calls* pizza), but one bad choice of a friend might. It won't necessarily kill us in body like it could have killed Linda, but it could kill us in spirit. If you choose friends who're always depressed, you could become a real bummer to be around. If you choose sarcastic friends, you might develop a sharp tongue.

Picking and Reaping

What kind of friends do you have? The Bible says you should pick your friends carefully because you'll become like them. In Proverbs, wise Solomon says,

> Whoever walks with the wise will become wise;
> whoever walks with fools will suffer harm. *(13:20, NLT)*

Maybe the friends you have right now won't be yours for life, but the type of friends you choose will set a pattern for the rest of your life.

Hanging Out Together

Write down the names of two of your closest friends. What kind of reputations do they have?

Friend   *Reputation*

_____   _____

_____   _____

_____   _____

According to Proverbs 13:20, are any of these relationships harmful? What are you going to do about those that are?

_____

_____

Remember that the friends you choose affect who you become down the road. If God were standing next to you now, would he be pleased with the friends you hang out with? Why or why not?

_____

_____

Maximum FRIENDSHIP

Week Five
A Walk in Your Shoes

Maximum FRIENDSHIP

Maximum FRIENDSHIP

DAY ONE
Who's Better?

Thursday night, midnight—the end of the semester. Andy got up from his chair, stretched, and yawned. It was high-pressure time for Andy. His brain felt like cottage cheese.

The next morning his best friend Mark roared over in his Jeep to pick him up. "You're the best!" Andy yelled and grinned at Mark, stretched out in his old four-wheeler.

"Yeah, I know, old man," Mark replied. "Hey, did you study for old Laver's test?"

"A lot. I gotta do well on it or I won't get into Edison next year." Andy sighed.

"Are you kidding?" Mark exploded. "I didn't even review the stuff. It'll be a cinch!" Andy couldn't believe it. Of course, Mark was a real brain and all, but not study?

The test was tough, a real hair-twister. Andy got a C-. Guess what Mark got? An A! He aced it. Andy felt sick. It was the old I'm-not-as-smart-as-him-but-I-wish-I-were problem. Why did he have to work so much harder than Mark just to pass? Suddenly, Andy felt a cold stab of jealousy.

Pass or Fail?

There's always someone who's better than you. If you're the smartest kid in your school, then the kid from your rival school is smarter. Or maybe you're a whiz at math but impossibly dumb at English literature. Maybe you're a klutz and wish you were like Joe Athletic. No matter who you are or what age you are or where you live, someone will always be better than you.

An Old Problem

Saul, in the Old Testament, had the same problem. He was a great king, with all the wealth and position you could ever want. But guess who he was jealous of? A shepherd/servant boy named David, who went into battle and fought *for* Saul.

Then it got even worse. When David marched back from battle, the people sang, "Saul killed his thousands but David his ten thousands." David killed at least ten times as many people as Saul. And because of jealousy, Saul tried to kill David. Why? You see, on their test, David got an A and Saul only a C-.

You're the One Who Counts

Even though James lived a long time ago, he hit the nail on the head when he wrote about jealousy:

> For where you have envy and selfish ambition, there you find disorder and every evil practice. But the wisdom that comes from heaven is first of all pure; then peace-loving, considerate, submissive, full of mercy and good fruit, impartial and sincere. Peacemakers who sow in peace raise a harvest of righteousness.
> *James 3:16-18*

It doesn't matter how well you do compared to someone else. What *does* count is what you do and think in relation to yourself. If you try your hardest and have a good attitude no matter what you do, then you've passed the test with an A+.

Name one person you're jealous of (whether it's because of clothes, money, social status, beauty, whatever). Also write down why you feel jealous.

_____

_____

The next time you see that person, remind yourself that God loves you—just the way you are.

DAY TWO
Hey, Did You Hear About . . . ?

Jim and Eliot were "soul-bro's." At least Jim thought so. Then one day Jim overheard Eliot telling something personal about him in the locker room. Two weeks ago Jim had finally gotten up enough guts to ask Rachel out. She was a really sweet girl, and Jim liked her a lot.

The way Eliot told the story, it sounded like Jim and Rachel had made out in the back seat. Jim was disgusted—and steaming! It wasn't even true. Of course, he knew that Eliot loved to add color and details to stories, but he never thought Eliot would ever do something like that to him.

Standing there in his underwear, Jim felt more than naked. Eliot had betrayed him. He wondered what he should do about it.

Jim didn't have to wonder long. By the afternoon, the whole school knew "the facts"—what they thought were facts anyway. Old Broadcast Mouth Brenda, who had a megaphone for a voice, had done her job on the gossip hotline well.

The Gossip Hotline
Is all really fair in friendship and war? Or are there rules? Sometimes we wonder—especially when someone betrays us. The gossip hotline is not only news—it's *bad* news. The Bible has a lot to say about it (see Proverbs 26:17-28 for some colorful examples of how God feels about gossips).

More to the Story
Samson was a guy who felt betrayed. You see, he met this girl

Delilah—the #1 two-faced woman. Delilah was gorgeous, a real babe. Every guy was drooling over her. Well, Delilah took special interest in Samson, who was also a good-looking hunk of a guy, and he *really* liked her. A tough guy, Samson had only one weakness—pretty women. And Delilah knew it.

But there is more to the story. Actually Delilah was just pretending to like Samson so she could get a secret out of him, the secret of his strength. Her persistence won, and she got what she wanted. Then she told the people who had hired her.

What was the result? Samson's long hair was chopped off, his eyes were blinded, and he was chained and tossed into prison. Eventually a building fell on him and crushed him to death.

Most likely none of you will go through what Samson did. But sometimes you might feel like a building fell right on you. You can't believe someone has betrayed you—especially if you thought he or she was your friend.

One of the most powerful tools we have is the human tongue. Even though the tongue is a small part of the human body, it is extremely hard to tame (see James 3:8). What comes out of our mouth can be one of two things—encouraging, or destroying. Paul gives us some guidelines:

> Do not let any unwholesome talk come out of your mouths, but only what is helpful for building others up according to their needs, that it may benefit those who listen. *Ephesians 4:29*

Taming the Tongue

When Old Broadcast-Mouth Brenda tells you some sizzling news about someone in school, think about three things before you pass it on: *Is it true? Is it kind? Does it have to be said?*

Think of a situation where you or someone you know was betrayed. How did you feel then? Now?

_____

_____

What did you do about it? What do you think Christ would have done about it?

_____

_____

The next time you hear gossip, walk in Christ's sandals and set the example.

DAY THREE
Used and Abused

Math brain! Nerd! Ryan could tell that's what they were thinking as he walked down the hall toward his calculus room. Sure, he looked the part with his glasses, calculator, and stack of notebooks and textbooks. He couldn't help being a math genius. Neither could his dad—it ran in the family.

Today he'd been surprised to find his favorite, a Snickers, taped to his door with a note that said, "From an admirer." Wow! he thought. The rest of the day he whizzed around the school, humming to himself. The next day he found another chocolate bar—he couldn't believe his luck! On Thursday morning there was a big Hershey's kiss tied with a bow. Now he knew someone was in love with him.

Then he found out who it was. Carleen—a popular girl who was dumb in math. She walked up to him and said, "Hey, how'd you like your notes? I wanted to see if you could come over to my house tonight."

"Sure," Ryan said, grinning. "Meet you after school?" That night Carleen poured on the sweet talk. He helped her finish her math assignment and then gave her tips on what to study for the test.

Friday's math test was hard. After it was all over, Ryan walked up to Carleen and asked, "Hey, how'd you do?"

"Great with all your help!" she replied. But somehow, by looking at her and seeing the little sweet-as-sour-grapes smirk she gave her friends, Ryan's heart sank. He felt used.

People Aren't Things

All of us have felt used at some time in our lives. And we've probably made others feel that way. Somehow we get things mixed up: instead of using things and loving people, we love things and use people.

Catching the Hypocrite

God protects human dignity. He encourages us to be truthful:

> Put off your old self, which is being corrupted by its deceitful desires . . . Therefore each of you must put off falsehood and speak truthfully to his neighbor, for we are all members of one body. *Ephesians 4:22, 25*

Carleen was a hypocrite—someone who pretended to be and do one thing, but actually was and did another. She led poor Ryan to believe she was interested in him just to get a good grade on a math test. Then she dropped him. And to make his humiliation worse, she did it in front of her friends.

'Fessing Up

Think about and complete the following sentences.

I wasn't really truthful when I _____.

Instead of caring about him/her, I had my own best interests in mind when I _____.

Think about how you could have acted differently and spoken truth in those situations. You might want to pray the following prayer:

Jesus, I'm sorry I used (name)_____. Please give me courage to apologize to _____, and remind me in the future that hypocrisy hurts both that person and me. Help me to grow to be the kind of friend that you want me to be. Amen.

DAY FOUR
Superiority Scene

Best *friend? Yeah, sure!* Sandy muttered, as Allison bounced off with the other cheerleaders in her short blue and white skirt. It had happened again—just like she knew it would.

Sandy and Allison had been forever-friends at Franklin High. They'd been friends for so long that the other kids at school teased them about living in the same skin.

This year was different. Allison had made varsity cheerleader and she was excited. But life was downhill into bumsville for Sandy. Allison looked cute the first pep rally of the year in her outfit, flinging around her pompoms. Suddenly everyone wanted Allison around. No one seemed to notice Sandy, who felt like sinking right through the mint green walls. But that wasn't too bad—she still had Allison.

By November, though, Allison didn't have time for Sandy anymore. Whenever they made plans, Allison got a better offer, and off she went. She still *acted* like Sandy's best friend when she had time to be, but Allison didn't make much time for Sandy anymore. And when she did, she kept talking about what she did with the other cheerleaders and football players and how terrific it was to be part of the in-crowd.

She thinks I'm not good enough for her anymore! Sandy thought. Ooh—that hurt! *After all these years, how could she? Wasn't their friendship worth something?* Sandy felt like a worm squished on a sidewalk.

It's Your Choice

When Allison made the varsity squad and started meeting new people, she made a choice about how she'd treat Sandy and her other old friends. But Allison got caught up in the excitement of pep rallies and games and forgot to be sensitive to Sandy.

Joseph of the Old Testament also experienced some new, unexpected privileges. First, he was his dad's favorite. And he, like Allison, wasn't very sensitive to his brothers. He strutted around in his special coat and bragged about strange dreams of superiority over them.

I'm Better than You

Later, after years of slavery and imprisonment, Joseph had another opportunity to lord it over his jealous brothers. This time he really was high and mighty (he had become Pharaoh's #1 assistant and governor of all Egypt), but he didn't act superior to his brothers. He never once said, "I'm better than you!" Instead he lovingly showed them that he considered them part of his "in-crowd," even after the bad things they'd done to him over the years.

Where Do You Fit in the Game?

Have you ever felt like someone was putting the superiority scene over on you? How did that make you feel?

_____

_____

Are you lording it over anyone (it could be a next-door neighbor kid who's pesky, a new person at school, or a brother or sister)? If so, who?

_____

_____

Tell that person this week that you've wronged them and that you're sorry. Ask a good friend to tell you if you're acting superior. And remember that the Bible says:

> Live in harmony with one another. Do not be proud, but be willing to associate with people of low position. Do not be conceited. *Romans 12:16*

DAY FIVE
The Big Letdown

Kevin was sweating it out. The history final was tough—he basically had to write a survey of everything he'd learned that semester. Whew!

He looked over at his friend T.J., grinned, and gave him the thumbs-up sign. Studying hard was paying off; he knew this stuff. But T.J. looked panic-stricken.

Kevin concentrated on his test. Just as he was two-thirds through, he felt someone's eyes on him. It was T.J. He had scooted his desk over a bit and was eye-balling Kevin's answers.

Kevin couldn't believe it! His buddy T.J. was cheating—and off his test. Moving his arm closer to his test, Kevin blocked T.J.'s view. But then he saw T.J. mouth wordlessly, *Come on, man!* Uncovering his test, Kevin started writing again. But his heart was heavy; he didn't even want to be T.J.'s friend anymore.

Not Perfect
Maybe, like Kevin, you've discovered people aren't perfect. Kevin couldn't believe T.J. would cheat, especially when they were both Christians. But even Christians aren't perfect. God calls us to be the light of the world (Matthew 5:14), but sometimes our lights flicker. As we try to become more like Christ, we realize how tough it is to be a Christian on our own. We need Jesus—and his power—to help us.

Classic Examples
Jesus' disciples—a perfect group, right? Look again. Peter was a loudmouthed fisherman who denied Christ when things got too hot

for him; Thomas questioned everything; John was a hot-head; Judas wanted to change the world with a revolution, and then when things didn't go his way, he betrayed his friends and later killed himself. The disciples were only too human, yet God used them to make big steps toward his kingdom. Paul described the goal of our lives this way:

> Not that I have already obtained all this, or have already been made perfect, but I press on to take hold of that for which Christ Jesus took hold of me. Brothers, I do not consider myself yet to have taken hold of it. But one thing I do: Forgetting what is behind and straining toward what is ahead, I press on toward the goal to win the prize for which God has called me heavenward in Christ Jesus. *Philippians 3:12-14*

Do you know who Paul was before he became Paul the apostle? He was Saul, the murderer of Christians. Yet God changed his life around so that he could tell others about Jesus.

Getting Over a Letdown
Has someone ever let you down? If so, what was the situation? And how did you handle it?

_____

_____

_____

If the same situation happened today, would you handle it any differently? If so, how?

_____

_____

_____

Have *you* ever let yourself or someone else down? Whenever you feel discouraged about your failures, remember that just as God transformed the lives of his disciples, he can change yours, too. Remember this verse in the tough times:

> You, dear children, are from God and have overcome them, because the one who is in you is greater than the one who is in the world. *1 John 4:4*

Week Six
Nasty Little Papercuts

DAY ONE
Enduring the "Dump"

Bianca and Corey were best friends. That summed them up well. Ever since they'd both moved here in fifth grade, they had been inseparable. Even their parents were friends.

One day Bianca was walking down the hall when she spied Corey. "Hey, Cor, want to get ice cream after school? Mom gave me some extra money."

Shock set in when Corey retorted, "Ice cream? Are you kidding? That's kid stuff. I'm going out with Lisa and Annette to *Denmark* Mall." She stressed *Denmark,* a fashionable mall on the expensive side of town.

On the way home, Bianca's pace was much slower than usual. When she got to her room, she felt empty. Corey usually walked home with her.

The next day Bianca decided to forget it and just approach Corey as if nothing had happened. But she didn't have the chance. Just before class started, she spied Corey down the hallway. As she rushed down to meet her, Corey looked at Bianca coldly for a minute, then dismissed her with a quick wave that said *Go away.*

Her body shaking, Bianca backed off and made her way to the restroom before the tears started to flow. She didn't even hear the bell when it rang.

Tough Squeeze
Poor Bianca. She felt like David had: "Even my best friend, the one I trusted completely, the one who shared my food, has turned against me" (Psalm 41:9, NLT). Even though only one person had

slam-dunked her, Bianca's world had caved in. Her heart felt like someone was squeezing the blood out of it. *I just don't understand!* she cried.

On a Desert Island

Jesus knew what it was like to be deserted. Peter denied him three times and ran off to save his own hide. And to top it off, most of his friends deserted him when he was nailed to the cross. Jesus understands when you feel like you're on a desert island—and someone has stolen all the life boats.

Band-aids

David wrote some psalms while he was running in fear for his life. He felt deserted—and betrayed—by all those he loved. And yet he had a champion wound-healer:

> The LORD hears his people when they call to him for help.
> He rescues them from all their troubles.
> The LORD is close to the brokenhearted;
> he rescues those who are crushed in spirit.
> The righteous face many troubles,
> but the LORD rescues them from each and every one.
> *Psalm 34:17-19, NLT*

Has someone ever wounded or betrayed you? How did it make you feel?

_____

_____

Think about when you may have wounded someone else. How can the way you've felt when you were hurt or betrayed help you relate in love to the person you've hurt?

_____

_____

If you're wearing someone's foot mark on your face today, ask Jesus to give you new hope so you can pick up and carry on.

DAY TWO
The Great Blow-off

Guys' *Night Out! Whoopee!* Ron high-slapped the door frame and raced out the door. He'd been waiting a long time for this. A month ago, he and Jeff had planned to do the night up big together—just the two of them.

At 6:00, as Ron was pulling on his Levi's, Jeff called. "Hey, bud! Would you mind if I brought Dan along tonight?"

Ron froze. "I thought you said it'd be the two of us."

"Yeah, I know. But I already told Dan he could come along," Jeff replied.

Ron told him he guessed it was okay and hung up. Furious, he paced in front of the mirror. *Just great! I knew it wouldn't work out. Dan* would *have to come—tonight.*

That night at the movies, it was so packed they could find only two seats together. So Ron sat by himself a few rows down. Afterwards they went out for tacos. Jeff and Dan were still talking about tai chi practice, and since Ron didn't know anything about it, he kept his mouth shut. He felt like a pesky insect.

Mosquitoes Are Pests
At some time in our lives, we've all felt like pests. Whether people are actually slapping at us or not, we feel that they are. It isn't easy to get hyped about something and then be disappointed. Ron felt blown-off—like he wasn't important enough to be around. If Jeff and Dan weren't trying to ignore him, they had a strange way of showing it.

Revenge Isn't All It's Cracked Up to Be

Getting back at them for being such snobs was the first thing on Ron's mind—a very human response. When we're hurt, we want revenge. We want to make someone else pay for hurting us. And it doesn't matter if "paying for it" is physical or emotional. The old saying, "Sticks and stones may break my bones but words can never hurt me" isn't true. *Verbal* pay-back is as hurtful as physical abuse. And it happens a lot in families, even Christian ones. Paul warns us in Romans 12:17-21:

> Do not repay anyone evil for evil. Be careful to do what is right in the eyes of everybody. If it is possible, as far as it depends on you, live at peace with everyone. Do not take revenge, my friends, but leave room for God's wrath, for it is written: "It is mine to avenge; I will repay," says the Lord.
>
> On the contrary: "If your enemy is hungry, feed him; if he is thirsty, give him something to drink. In doing this, you will heap burning coals on his head." Do not be overcome by evil, but overcome evil with good.

That's a tough Scripture to read when you're angry, but it's true. Thinking of ways to get revenge only hurts *us,* because we're dwelling on it. But when we let go of our anger, we're free of it.

Pest Control

When have you felt like a pesky insect to someone else? What did you do about it?

_____

_____

Have you ever treated anyone else like a pest? Think back and be honest.

_____

_____

Ask Christ to put his forgiveness in your heart toward those who've wronged you and give you his love and understanding toward those you've wronged.

DAY THREE
It Takes Guts

Remember Ron, Jeff, and Dan? Well, Ron stayed angry for over a week at Jeff. After all, it was pretty mean of Jeff to ignore him all night and spend time with Dan (who wasn't supposed to be invited anyway).

Jeff acted normal around Ron, and that made Ron even angrier. Finally, he'd had it with Jeff. Jeff had to know that he had hurt him. Ron decided to talk with him. The problem was getting him alone. A popular guy, Jeff always had a crowd around him. Ron finally captured him after fifth period.

"Hey, man, I need to talk with you," Ron said hesitantly.

"Sure! Do you want to grab the bench after school? I've got half an hour before I have to be at practice," Jeff gushed.

As soon as the end-of-the-day bell rang, Ron leaped out of his seat. This thing was bugging him, and he wanted it resolved. Ron told Jeff how he'd felt that night and was feeling now. Jeff was astounded. "I didn't know you felt like that, Ron! I just thought it would be nice to invite Dan since he was new at school and all. I didn't know it would hurt your feelings."

After they talked, Ron felt so relieved. Jeff liked him and was really a nice guy after all!

Fairy-Tale Ending

Maybe you're thinking to yourself, *"That's a fairy-tale ending. No macho guy would admit to that."* Sure, not all endings to problems work out that easily, but we at least have to try. It *can* happen that way. Christ holds us responsible to live in harmony with others because as Christians we're to be role models of him to others.

I Just Can't!

Maybe you're saying, "But I've really been hurt. You don't understand how I feel or you couldn't ask me to go to that jerk!" Maybe someone has backbitten you, blabbed something they shouldn't have, or made up a lie about you. But Christ still holds us responsible to go to that person. He wants no division between his children. God wants us to be at peace in our relationships. Through the apostle Paul's words God calls us to live this way:

> If anyone has caused grief he has not so much grieved me as he has grieved all of you [in the church], . . . Now instead, you ought to forgive and comfort him, so that he will not be overwhelmed by excessive sorrow. I urge you, therefore, to reaffirm your love for him. *2 Corinthians 2:5-8*

If you feel or cause sorrow, Christ also feels it. And the rest of the body of Christ feels it, because we are all parts of one unified body.

I Can

Confronting someone takes a lot of guts. Whether we're the ones who've been hurt, or the ones who've done the hurting, God can give us the power to make the first step. Is there someone you should approach today? Write the name here and then list some positive qualities about this person (even if it's tough to do right now).

_____

_____

When you talk with him or her, first share the good qualities you appreciate about that person. People are more willing to listen if you compliment them first before presenting the problem.

Christ says in Philippians 4:13: "I can do everything through him who gives me strength." Ask Christ to help you swallow your ego and to give you gutsy courage.

DAY FOUR
When You Mess Up

Kathy sank into the blue leather couch. *I've made such a mess of things! And it's all my fault!* She knew that no one else could get her out of what she had done. This one topped the charts.

Erika had only been at Churchill High for six weeks after moving there from California. As far as Kathy knew, she was an only child. Since Kathy and Erika both played flute in band, they hit it off immediately. After spending lots of time with Kathy, Erika had dropped a bombshell.

Erika and Kathy had been munching peanut butter cookies in the kitchen. Then Erika said, "Can I tell you something? Can you keep a secret?"

Kathy felt privileged that Erika wanted to tell her. "Sure," she said, without giving it a second thought.

"Well, there's something I've been wanting to tell you for a long time. You see, I do have a brother—back in California. He's nine years older than me, and—" Her voice slowed to a whisper. "Well, he's gay, and he lives with another guy." Kathy was shocked. Sure, she knew that some people were gay, but she never knew anyone whose *brother* was gay.

A couple of weeks later at school, Kathy and some of her friends were talking. Somehow, they got on the subject of gay people. All of a sudden, before she realized it, Erika's secret had slipped out. It didn't take long to get around school, and the kids started to make fun of Erika. Kathy felt responsible—and she was.

When There's No Eraser

Kathy's stuck in an awful position. After ruining someone's life and reputation, there's not much she can do to repair it. It's like poking someone's eye out; there's nothing you can do to make that eye grow back. Kathy can't erase that news from the minds or memories of the kids at Churchill High. She's miserable.

White-Out

Kathy can't change the circumstances, but she does need to confess her sin: "If we confess our sins, he is faithful and just and will forgive us our sins and purify us from all unrighteousness" (1 John 1:9).

Confessing our sins to God is like taking a bottle of white-out to them. They're gone forever from God's book. But we must do more than just confess our sin to God.

Not only must Kathy confess her sin to God and say she's sorry, but she must take action. First she must admit to Erika that what she did was wrong, and that she's very sorry. Then she must ask Erika to forgive her. Finally she must forgive herself (which is perhaps the hardest of the three things to do). We'll talk more about these steps in the upcoming days.

Wiping Up the Mess

Kathy can't change what happened, but she can change her reaction to it. She can mope around and say, "I'm such a loser." Or she can realize she's made a mistake and do what she can to make it right with Erika by defending her in front of the other students.

Have you ever made a mess of something? What?

_____

_____

If you've hurt someone else, contact that person. If he or she won't talk with you, leave a special note on his or her locker. Or bake something to show you care about their hurt. Read David's psalm for encouragement today:

Praise the LORD, O my soul,
   and forget not all his benefits—
who forgives all your sins,
   and heals all your diseases,
who redeems your life from the pit
   and crowns you with love and compassion.
Psalm 103:2-4

DAY FIVE
Healing the Wound—for Good

Again we meet Kathy and Erika. But this time, let's look at Erika's side.

Erika was embarrassed and upset when all the kids started poking fun at her saying things like, "If your brother's gay, are you a lesbian?" Then they'd skitter off down the hall, laughing.

But what really crushed her was that she'd trusted Kathy with her deepest secret. How could Kathy have told anyone? Kathy tried to talk to her at school, but Erika just ignored her and walked on by. And when Kathy called her at home, Erika didn't return her calls. Finally, though, a month later, Erika was so lonely she agreed to hear what Kathy had to say—by phone.

Kathy poured out her story in tears and said how sorry she was. Up till now, Erika had seen her as an enemy. Suddenly she seemed human—she hurt just like Erika.

But still Erika couldn't forgive her—Kathy had ruined her life, and she could never trust her again. So after mumbling on the line, "I'm sorry, I really don't want to talk with you," Erika hung up.

70 x 7

Forgiveness is hard to give—especially when it's your neck in the noose. It's even harder when the person who fails you was someone you trusted.

When Peter asked Jesus, "Lord, how many times shall I forgive my brother when he sins against me? Up to seven times?" (Matthew 18:21), Peter thought he was being saintly and generous. He was shocked at Jesus' response, "Seventy times seven." It blew him away.

Scar Tissue

Ending a conflict is as hard as keeping New Year's resolutions. Old scars keep showing up red at the surface. But Scripture challenges us:

Let us therefore make every effort to do what leads to peace and to mutual edification. *Romans 14:19*

And the writer of Hebrews encourages us with the way God forgives:

For I will forgive their wickedness and will remember their sins no more. *Hebrews 8:12*

Our task is pretty clear . . . to forgive and forget. Two very simple, but difficult words.

A Super-Human Dose

Do you need to forgive someone? Why?

_____

_____

In your prayer time today, ask for God's forgiveness. Ask him to help you forgive yourself. Then contact the person you're having problems with. Be sincere and honest. Whether he or she accepts your efforts or not, you'll know you've obeyed God. And you can commit the rest of the process to him.

Week Seven
Buddies No Matter What

DAY ONE
Are Old People Really Human?

Tia leaned back against the warm sofa and sniffed her steaming hot chocolate. *This is such a wonderful place,* she sighed, and snuggled into the creamy afghan. Coming here once a week was always worth the five-block walk—even in the middle of a winter like this one.

*Mrs. Madge—no, Martha—*she reminded herself (because that's what Mrs. Madge had asked Tia to call her) *was a terrific lady.* She seemed to care a lot about the high school kids she taught, more than just the average, everyday English teacher.

One day when Tia was feeling down, Martha had noticed and had invited her over to her house after school. Martha thought of everything—even calling Tia's mom so she wouldn't be worried. During their talk, Tia discovered that Martha's husband had died a year ago and that she was lonely.

At first Tia started visiting Martha once a week because—well—she felt rather sorry for her. But by December, things had changed drastically. Tia looked forward to their time together eagerly. Martha was the first older lady she *wanted* to spend time with. Martha giggled over Tia's jokes, loved chocolate (especially gooey, half-baked brownies—Tia's favorite), and comforted her when she'd had a bad day.

For the first time in her life, Tia had a true friend she could share with—the good things as well as the bad. Martha understood. Tia only wished that they'd found each other earlier.

Family Friends

Believe it or not, Tia and Martha aren't the only people in the history of the world to have an unusual relationship like that. Ruth and Naomi are another shining example. Naomi was Ruth's mother-in-law, but the old adage of mother-in-law-not-getting-along-with-the-wife didn't come true here. Even as family members, they had an incredible friendship.

When Ruth's husband died, Ruth didn't leave Naomi to remarry. Naomi was a widow, too, and Ruth stayed to be a loving support because Naomi was alone. This was unusual because outside of marriage, women had no place in that culture and they usually re-married. Because of her love for Naomi, Ruth endured being an outsider who had no protection from a husband.

God blessed Ruth for her friendship with the older woman. He gave her a wonderful home and husband, and blessed Naomi with grandchildren in her old age. Eventually, King David would be Ruth's great grandson!

Disciple-making

Paul the apostle had an unusual relationship with Timothy, whom he called "my beloved son." From reading Paul's letters in 1 and 2 Timothy, we can gather the following information about Timothy: he was a young man, a young Christian, timid and weak in his faith, and he wasn't physically well. Although they were miles away from each other, Paul wrote him two specific, lengthy letters encouraging him to stand strong in his faith and to rekindle his desire to serve God.

Bridging the Gap

Be friends with an older person? *You've got to be kidding*, you might say. *I have nothing in common with them, and besides, they wouldn't understand me. Everybody knows there's a big gap between adults and teens.*

Perhaps there is a gap between *some* teens and *some* adults, but who says there has to be? There are a lot of things teens can learn from older people. Solomon, the world's wisest man, encourages teens to: "Listen to counsel and accept discipline, that you may be wise the rest of your days" (Proverbs 19:20).

And—surprise—there are many wonderful things adults can learn from teens: a renewed zest for life, a different vocabulary, and some ideas for creative fun, to mention a few. Just think what a terrific relationship you and an older person may be missing!

Write down the name of an older person you could pursue a friendship with. (Or if you can't think of any, make a quick visit to a nursing home; you'd be surprised what spunky older people you'll find!)

_____

_____

Now write down an activity you could do for an hour with this older person. (It could be watching a video, cooking dinner together, looking over scrapbooks or photo albums, playing miniature golf, etc. The list is endless!) Give yourself one week to carry out your plan.

_____

_____

If the idea of getting together with an older person scares you somewhat, here's some encouragement from Jeremiah:

"Do not say, 'I am only a child.' You must go to everyone I send you to and say whatever I command you. Do not be afraid of them, for I am with you and will rescue you," declares the LORD. *Jeremiah 1:7-8*

DAY TWO
Hopscotch Is Kid Stuff

L eah, I'm over here!" Jerry called and ducked behind the sofa in the Children's Care Center. Leah chortled and scampered in his direction as quickly as her chubby five-year-old legs could carry her.

The change in her was incredible. Two weeks ago, Leah had been abandoned on the steps of the Center where Jerry worked after school. At first she just gently rocked on the floor with her fists clenched tightly in her lap. She would sit head-down like that for hours. Then one day, Leah surprised Jerry by climbing into his lap. She looked at him, her blue eyes large with questions until he hugged her.

After that day, Jerry and Leah were buddies. Jerry spent even more volunteer time than usual at the center. Somehow he surprised himself: *I can't believe it. I really care about these kids!*

His work was no longer just a job.

#1 in God's Eyes
It's easy to think that children are just kids—little rug rats, curtain climbers, things that get in our way and under our feet. But Jesus loved children and thought highly of them.

When some children were brought to Jesus so he could pray for them, the disciples rebuked them and were going to send them away. But Jesus said, "Let the little children come to me, and do not hinder them, for the kingdom of heaven belongs to such as these" (Matthew 19:14). Jesus didn't think that children were bothersome; he took time to love them and pray for them.

Who's the Greatest?

When Jesus talked affectionately with his disciples, he called them "children." And he gave them a big lesson about faith. When the disciples rallied around Jesus, asking who the greatest one would be in the kingdom of heaven, Jesus brought a child before them and said:

> "I tell you the truth, unless you change and become like little children, you will never enter the kingdom of heaven. There-fore, whoever humbles himself like this child is the greatest in the kingdom of heaven. And whoever welcomes a little child like this in my name welcomes me." *Matthew 18:3-5*

By now, the disciples' mouths were hanging open in shock. A kid—*the greatest?* In those days, children were seen but not heard; they had no rights. So Jesus' teaching stunned the disciples. But they were even more astonished when Jesus continued to say that chil-dren were so important that it would be better for someone to drown than hurt them!

Focus on Kids

How much time do you spend with children? In what situations?

_____

_____

Is the time you spend with children *voluntary* or something you feel you have to do? (For instance, do you go to your five-year-old cousin's birthday party just because your mom is making you? Do you babysit just to get extra cash when underneath it all you *hate* kids?)

The next time you're with children, whether it's your choice or not, use your time to shine as a light for God. Remember—what you say and do is extremely important to a child because he will look up to you as a role model. Ask God to give you a loving heart for those kids around you.

DAY THREE
You're Not Just My Brother

It was 4:00 A.M. Nina paced back and forth in front of the bay window. Every two minutes, she parted the curtains and peered through into the rainy blackness.

"Where is he? He should be here by now!" she said out loud, but really more to herself.

It was Friday night—no, early Saturday morning—and Nina was downright worried about her brother Joel. He was never late for anything. Because it was Nina's sixteenth birthday tomorrow, he was coming from Rockville College just to celebrate. And he'd promised her a ride in the fiery red Corvette he'd just bought from another guy at college.

Nina had tried to fall asleep on the couch, but she just couldn't— except for short snatches. Every time she heard voices, or a car door slam, she woke up with a start. But by 4:00, she was bolt awake. Visions of all the horrible things that might have happened to him flew through her mind. Maybe he'd stopped to get gas, and someone stole his car, or—even more horrible—maybe he'd fallen asleep at the wheel and *crashed!*

Nina thought back to the times that they'd fought as kids over toys and bicycles, and the snotty comments that she had made when he started shaving and wearing cologne. And then, there was the time in fifth grade when she got really mad and bit him because he read her diary!

Still, in spite of their little fights, Joel was a great brother. He really stuck up for her. *Kind of like a guardian angel,* Nina thought. Tears flooded her eyes.

Just then she heard a car door slam, and feet tripped up the stairs. *Joel!* Nina flung the door open and threw herself in her brother's arms.

For the first time in her life she realized that her brother was not just her brother—he was her friend.

Getting Along

Getting along isn't easy—especially when it's someone you have to be around all the time, like your family. Maybe it's that pesky younger brother who's always nagging you to fly kites with him (and you think that would be terribly uncool). Or perhaps your younger sister gets into everything—including your makeup, clothes, and personal journal! Or maybe your older brother is a real geek and does stupid things that embarrass you.

Somehow, it's hard for that "brotherly love in Christ" kind of feeling to stretch to your own relatives. Maybe you even wish that you had been born into a different family because your own is so weird!

Relative Power

The Bible gives us examples of people who were siblings and actually got along. Sure, it wasn't always easy, but they worked at their relationships.

Martha, Mary, and Lazarus are one such example. Martha and Mary were as different as any two people could be—Martha ran her legs off, trying to be the perfect hostess when Jesus came because she wanted to make sure things were just right. Mary, on the other hand, wanted to spend time with Jesus, so she hung around, right by his feet. And the result? Martha got mad at Mary, called her a lazy bum, and complained to Jesus about it. Undoubtedly, that wasn't the only sisterly incident like that. But even though Martha and Mary had lots of differences to work through, they shared two common loves—their brother Lazarus, and Jesus Christ. When Lazarus died, they both mourned his death and begged Jesus to heal him. What a family celebration there must have been when Lazarus walked out of his grave, with the graveclothes streaming from him!

Take Your Home's Temperature

First John 3:10 warns, "This is how we know who the children of God are and who the children of the devil are: Anyone who does not do what is right is not a child of God; nor is anyone who does not love his brother." In short, God is saying that anyone who does not love his brother or sister—and that includes siblings—is not his child. Christ calls us to treat our family members with love and respect, and wants us to keep harmony in our homes.

How do you treat your other family members? Make notes about your individual relationship with each one of them.

_____

_____

Is there a family member you're having problems with? If so, jot down some ideas about how you can make peace with him or her.

_____

_____

During your prayer time today, read the following verses. Then ask God to help you live them out:

> As a prisoner for the Lord, then, I urge you to live a life worthy of the calling you have received. Be completely humble and gentle; be patient, bearing with one another in love. Make every effort to keep the unity of the Spirit through the bond of peace. *Ephesians 4:1-3*

DAY FOUR
People Who Grow on You—Like Fungus

For weeks, Trent, the Geek of Scobey High, had been following Deanna around the school halls. No matter where she was—class, her locker, right outside the girls' restroom—he showed up. With his plastic glasses and pocket protector, he was a real nerdy-looking character. So far, Deanna had been pretty good at avoiding him. But today her luck had run out.

I can't believe it! Deanna thought. *He's such a geek! And why does he have to sit at my lunch table?* Carefully she lowered her orange tray with her milk and hamburger lunch special to the opposite end of the table. With a quick smile, she nodded to him and eased into the attachable bench seat.

I'm so glad Mary and Susan are on their way. Phew! Deanna sighed. But her relief was short-lived. In one clumsy act, Trent scooped up himself and his tray and swooped down next to her.

Oh no! This is so-o-o embarrassing! Deanna screamed inside. *I'd rather kiss my brother than sit next to this guy!* Her stomach flip-flopped. This was the worst day of her life.

Unlovable People

If you were Deanna, what would you do? Loving or even liking "unlovable" people is tough, especially when you feel like your popularity is on the line. After all, why should you put yourself out for a goof or a nerd, right? They can take care of themselves.

Jesus had to deal with unlovables. And even though he was perfect and sinless, he probably didn't always find it easy either. So he can identify with you—whether it's the girl in your math class who never washes her greasy hair, or the smelly guy whose locker is next to yours (sometimes you feel like putting a can of deodorant in his locker when he's not looking).

Partial People

The book of James talks a lot about attitudes and playing favorites:

> My dear brothers and sisters, how can you claim that you have faith in our glorious Lord Jesus Christ if you favor some people more than others?
>
> For instance, suppose someone comes into your meeting dressed in fancy clothes and expensive jewelry, and another comes in who is poor and dressed in shabby clothes. If you give special attention and a good seat to the rich person, . . . doesn't this discrimination show that you are guided by wrong motives? . . . "Love your neighbor as yourself." But if you pay special attention to the rich, you are committing a sin, for you are guilty of breaking that law. *James 2:1-4, 8-9, NLT*

Turning Garbage to Good

When Jesus met an adulterous woman (see John 8:1-11), he didn't roll his eyes and dump her like some soggy, smelly piece of garbage. Boldly he took her aside and listened to her problems. And finally he comforted her and gave her a new chance at life. He took her immoral, "garbagy" life and made it beautiful and clean.

Your Chance

Are there any people in your school who bug you? Who are they, and why do you see them that way?

_____

_____

What difference would it make in your attitudes and actions if you saw them as people whom God loves, and then treated them that way?

_____

_____

What can you do this week to extend Jesus' love to the "unlovables" in your school? Make it simple and practical (it could be writing them a note, eating lunch with them, or even sharing a simple, friendly "hello").

_____

_____

Remember to ask yourself: _Am I treating these people as Jesus would?_

DAY FIVE
Sharks or Non-Christians?

Rhonda darted past Dave with a quick "hi" and hurriedly rounded the corner into her home room. Gratefully, she sank onto the cold wood chair and plopped her books on the floor. *Whew! I just got out of that one!* She sighed deeply. She was so glad this was the end of the school year. And yet she was sad too—she liked Dave as a person. But lately things had been taking an unexpected turn; she felt something more for him.

Just then she heard a shuffling sound. There he was. Dave—Mr. Detective. "Hey, Rhonda. I'm really interested in this God stuff. Maybe I could go to your Bible study with you sometime?" Dave asked.

"Uh, yeah. That would be good," Rhonda blurted out. "But to-night's the last Bible study until fall."

"Great! I'll come tonight. I can even pick you up, O.K.?" Reluc-tantly, Rhonda agreed. After tonight, he'd think she was a religious freak, and he'd never want to talk with her again.

Which Do You Fear the Most?
Sharks or non-Christians? When a non-Christian approaches you, do you immediately scramble out of the water, or do you gulp and wait for the big bite? But are non-Christians really as deadly as they appear? Will they warp you and make you forget your Christianity, or worse yet, laugh at you? Maybe you're afraid you'd have to become their personal prayer warrior and pray them into getting saved. Or maybe you're worried that talking to them is a waste of time.

Even worse, like Rhonda, maybe you're attracted to that person and would love to go out with him or her on a date. *Would it really be so bad to date that cute guy?* you wonder. *He seems nice enough.*

DANGER—Beware

Christ calls us to go into all the world and share the good news. That means sharing it through your life—your words and actions to your biology lab partner. But God also warns us about the kinds of relationships we should *not* have with non-Christians.

Paul tells us that marrying non-Christians is out (2 Corinthians 6:14). But what about dating non-Christians? The Bible doesn't state in black and white that you should not date an unbeliever, but it *does* give directing principles. It talks about how the heart gets involved in relationships. And once you have that type of involvement, there's a lot of hurt in breaking it off—for both of you. Remember, the purpose of dating is not only to have fun and get to know more about others and yourself—it's also to point you toward a possible marriage partner. Second Corinthians 6:14 makes it clear:

> Don't team up with those who are unbelievers. How can goodness be a partner with wickedness? How can light live with darkness? *(NLT)*

Jesus – 1; Sharks – 0

When Jesus died on the cross, he triumphed over Satan. He is only awaiting the final victory. And because we are his children we can claim his power—even in relating to non-Christians:

> No, in all these things we are more than conquerors through him who loved us. *Romans 8:37*

> Do not be afraid or discouraged because of this vast army. For the battle is not yours, but God's. *2 Chronicles 20:15*

So, the battle is already won! All we have to do is show up every day for service, knowing that Christ has already triumphed. What could be better?

What kinds of relationships do you have with non-Christians? What could you do to draw a non-Christian friend closer to God?

_____

_____

What do you need to steer clear of in your relationships with non-Christians, especially those of the opposite sex?

_____

_____

In your prayer time, thank God that, through Christ, he has already won our spiritual battle. Rejoice that he already has the death grip on Satan's neck. Ask him for courage to share your faith and to hold tightly to _his_ principles for godly relationships.

Week Eight
Jesus, the Ultimate Friend

DAY ONE
Best-Friend-of-the-Year Award

L ori and Bridget did everything together—like band and drama club and going out on weekends.

When Lori's boyfriend dumped her, Bridget was there. And Bridget and Lori cried together when Bridget's brother died in a car accident. They were two parts of the same heart; each could tell when the other one was hurting. And they could talk about anything, no matter how personal or embarrassing it was. They had perfect trust in each other.

Then Bridget's dad, who was an Army colonel, got transferred to Germany. Bridget and Lori cried together for a week. And then, suddenly, Bridget was gone. Lori clung to the photos of the two of them together, and to the stuffed raccoon that Bridget had left her. But the empty feeling remained. How she wished Bridget were here! She was so lonely.

It's not fair, God! Lori cried out. *She was my best friend in the whole world. I'll never find someone like her!* Still, months later, Lori's heart ached for her best friend.

Friends with God?

We've all lost friends at one time or another. But there's one friend who'll *never* leave us, who's continually there, who stands by our side no matter what. And just who is this Super Friend? God.

Maybe you're saying to yourself, *You've got to be kidding! No one can be friends with God. God's the guy who grabs a big stick and whaps you if you're not good. And, besides, you can't touch someone who isn't there—who doesn't have a body.*

If you're wondering what kind of "person" God really is, the best way to find out is to read the Bible. Think of it as a camera that takes God's photograph.

Focus on God

What makes God a good friend? He has all the qualities (and many, many more) of great friends that we've studied in this book—faithfulness, loyalty, a listening ear, someone who stays with us through tough times. But unlike human friends, God is always there. Just check out these verses, for starters:

> Do not be afraid or discouraged, for the LORD is the one who goes before you. He will be with you; he will neither fail you nor forsake you. *Deuteronomy 31:8, NLT*

> I still belong to you; you are holding my right hand. You will keep on guiding me with your counsel, leading me to a glorious destiny. *Psalm 73:23-24, NLT*

> God has said, "I will never fail you. I will never forsake you." That is why we can say with confidence, "The LORD is my helper, so I will not be afraid. What can mere mortals do to me?" *Hebrews 13:5-6, NLT*

Why not do your own search through Scripture to find out more about the kind of person God is?

Never Too Busy

Jesus is the best listener anyone could ever have. And he can be yours. In fact, he's listening right now for you to tell him your needs and desires. And the best thing of all is that his telephone line's always open. You'll never get a busy signal. And there are no toll charges.

How do *you* picture God? Write down some of his "qualities."

_____

_____

Do you see God as a friend and great listener, or as somebody who whacks you if you're not good? Why?

_____

_____

If you were getting to know someone, how would you accomplish that? Well, you'd probably talk with them—and then listen to what *they* say, right? In your prayer time today, ask God to show you what kind of a friend he really is. Get to know him better through talking with him and reading his words in the Bible.

DAY TWO
Somebody You Can't Shock

Just when everything was starting to go great again, John felt like quitting. After two years, he'd finally been interested in life again. A counselor had helped him climb out of the depression that had seemed to bury him.

He knew the peaceful, happy feeling was too good to last. Now it was happening all over again. He couldn't talk with his parents—they didn't pay much attention to him anymore. As far as they were concerned, John was "out of danger." They were sure he wouldn't embarrass them by trying to kill himself again.

John had met his buddy Steve at a volleyball game last summer. Steve was a cool guy, and he took a special interest in John. This year when John found out they'd be going to the same school, he was thrilled. He'd finally found a friend.

Or at least he'd thought so. Last week he'd shared his secret with Steve—what he had tried to do. Steve looked at him as if he were some kind of weirdo. But that wasn't all. Steve had promised he wouldn't tell anyone, but he'd let it slip to a couple of guys. Now they were all being so nice it was getting on John's nerves. He didn't want to feel like someone's "ministry."

Who Can You Trust?
John found out the hard way that not everyone can be trusted. He was bummed; he wondered if there was *anyone* in the world who could be trusted with the way he really felt and what he thought about.

All of us have felt like John did some time in our lives. Maybe it was when your best friend told a secret about you, or you found out the *real* reason somebody asked you out (it was on a dare called "Ask-the-Ugly-Out Night"). You were humiliated.

God's Upfront and Unshockable

Did you ever wish there was someone who knew you—and still loved you anyway? Someone who's never shocked? Someone who knows about the lies you told, the CD you stole from the store, or the gossip you passed on about a classmate at school? Somebody who knows your parents are having a tough time in life right now? We do have somebody like that—God. And Scripture proves it:

> Cast all your anxiety on him because he cares for you. And the God of all grace, who called you to his eternal glory in Christ, after you have suffered a little while, will himself restore you and make you strong, firm and steadfast. *1 Peter 5:7, 10*

As you open yourself up to God's love, you'll find new hope. Jesus accepts you just as you are. He understands your joys and hurts completely, even when others don't.

Open Hands

How do you feel about the fact that God knows you intimately? (Nervous, happy, uh-oh, I'm in trouble . . .)

_____

_____

Try doing this exercise during your prayer time. Write down anything that's bothering you today on a piece of paper. Crunch that paper into a ball in your fist. Then turn your palm up, still holding the wad of paper. Lift up your concerns to God in prayer; then turn your hand upside down and let the paper fall in the wastebasket.

That's how we can treat the things that are bothering us when we believe God cares about us and has control of everything in our lives. If we do that, the Bible tells us this: "If the Holy Spirit controls your mind, there is life and peace" (Romans 8:6, NLT). That's a great reward for giving up your concerns to God!

DAY THREE
When Life Isn't What You Expect

Tad swallowed hard. Sheila's words pounded over and over in his head: "Tad, I'm pregnant. What are we going to do?"

Sheila looked at him tearfully. Tad didn't know what to say. He never thought it would come to this—his parents would be shocked. After all, Tad was a PK—a preacher's kid. Everyone thought he was raised in a perfect home. They couldn't figure out what had gotten into him the last two years.

Tad caused his parents nothing but embarrassment. On his sixteenth birthday, he'd gone out drinking with his buddies. When the cops pulled them over for speeding, they'd found an open beer in the car. Tad had ended up in jail. His parents had picked him up, paid for his fines, and swallowed their pride.

But that wasn't the end. Tad was continually getting into a scrap of some sort. Last week he'd punched a guy out at school, and his weepy-eyed mother had to come to the principal's office on her lunch break.

Then there was Sheila, who was really a good kid. Her parents didn't care much for Tad—they thought he was pond scum and forbade her to go out with him anymore.

How am I going to tell my parents? Tad agonized. He knew they were going to fly off the handle and sock him. *Well, I deserve it,* he thought.

But he was surprised at their reaction: "Son," his father said slowly, "What you have done is wrong, very wrong. We have given you many chances to straighten yourself out, but you haven't tried. This baby is yours, and you've got two choices: marry Sheila now, or help her out with expenses and then agree together to give up the baby for adoption. Those are your choices. Now, son, it's up to you."

His parents turned and left the room. He heard his mother crying in the bedroom.

Rebel City

All of us know somebody *somewhat* like Tad. Maybe it's the gang-banger who goes to your high school and ends up in the principal's office every day. Or perhaps it's Tom, the guy who smokes marijuana in the parking lot at lunchtime. Or maybe it's Marsha, who doesn't know where she belongs, so she ends up in every guy's backseat at some time or another.

Being a teen isn't easy, especially if your parents aren't supportive of you. Maybe you think your mom has no brains at all, or that your dad doesn't love you. And that leads you to rebel against them—in the way you talk, dress, and act. Sometimes you don't know *why* you rebel.

Birthright

Esau was somewhat like Tad. He treated his "#1 son" status lightly. Genesis 25:34 tells the story of how Esau, home from a hunting trip, gave up his birthright (something permanent) for something temporary—stew for his hungry stomach.

In Bible times, the first-born son got special privileges, including the blessing of his father, for the rest of his life. He had his choice of everything. When Esau messed up, he could have gone to his father immediately and said, "Forgive me for picking something temporary over something eternal." But he didn't. Hebrews 12:15-17 tells us that Esau didn't repent.

Sold Out for God

Sometimes we as Christians can be like Tad and Esau. We take our Christian commitment too lightly. When we do something wrong, we go to God flippantly and pray, "Father, forgive me for what I did," and then we go back and do it again. We abuse our knowledge that God is a forgiving God. We don't seem to think we'll ever suffer the consequences of our sin.

Beware—there'll come a time when, like Tad and Esau, it will be too late. There'll be no chance to turn around. We may think we're getting away from our sin, but someday we'll suffer its consequences, like Tad and Sheila.

God wants us to be sold out for him. What does this mean? That when we do something wrong, we not only *confess* our sin and tell God we're sorry but also *forsake* our sin—turn away from it and refuse to do it again (see Psalm 51). Because God loves us, he'll confront us when we need to be confronted—even if our hearts are so hardened it takes a wallop instead of just a pin-prick.

Is there some area in *your* life where you have become hardened to doing wrong? A hidden place where you would be uncomfortable to bring Jesus with you? Write it down and tell God about it.

_____

_____

A right relationship with God requires that you spend time with God in prayer and reading his letter to you—the Bible. Why? Because it's more than just a book:

> All Scripture is inspired by God and is useful to teach us what is true and to make us realize what is wrong in our lives. It straightens us out and teaches us to do what is right. It is God's way of preparing us in every way, fully equipped for every good thing God wants us to do. *2 Timothy 3:16-17, NLT*

When life isn't what you expect, go to God. After all, if you've accepted Jesus Christ as your Savior, you *belong* to God, and you can trust him to know what's best for you at all times:

> And now, just as you accepted Christ Jesus as your Lord, you must continue to live in obedience to him. Let your roots grow

down into him and draw up nourishment from him, so you will grow in faith, strong and vigorous in the truth you were taught. Let your lives overflow with thanksgiving for all he has done. *Colossians 2:6-7, NLT*

DAY FOUR
Playin' Games

"Tony!" Tony turned just in time to see Doug dashing across his front lawn. "Dude, I'm glad I caught you. Do you want to go to a concert with me tomorrow? Dad's company got free tickets and he and Mom can't go," Doug wheezed, out of breath from his run.

"Sure, I'll go if you help me mow the lawn today. I promised I'd do it," Tony replied. Doug's fist tightened. He cared about Tony a lot, but sometimes Tony got to him. Tony always put conditions on everything so other people would help him out with his work. Still, he really wanted to go to the concert with Tony, so he agreed. They got the lawn done in a couple of hours.

The next night, Doug stopped over at Tony's house to pick him up for the concert. He was surprised to see Tony lounging around in his sweats.

"Oh!" Tony called. "I didn't know that the concert was tonight! Sorry! I can't go—I have to babysit for my little sister. Some other time."

Doug stormed out the door, furious. It was Tony's typical game. As soon as someone else helped him do his work, he canceled out on doing what they wanted to do. Doug had had it up to his ears with him. That was Tony's last chance, and he'd blown it.

Are Your Friends Conditional?

Has anyone ever played the game "Condition" with you? Things like—"I'll help you with your term paper if you'll come to my party tomorrow." "I'll like you if you get your hair cut the way I think you should." Or, "You really have to buy the coolest name-brand clothes to be a member of our crowd." How does that make you feel? Usually downright mad. Maybe, like Doug, you feel used, or that people are just looking on your outside and not on your inside. They want you to conform to being who *they* want you to be—not who you really are.

God's Condition

Unlike humans, God only puts one condition on his friendship— that you accept him into your life unconditionally. He wants to come in and transform you into the best person you can be. He won't play popularity games with you. You're either totally his, or you belong to Satan. There's no living in between the two.

God loved us so much that he sent his son Jesus to take all our sins on his back. Jesus died in agony on the cross, nails threading through his hands and feet. But he did it out of love and compassion for each one of us. Jesus gave his life because he created us and loved us immensely:

> The greatest love is shown when people lay down their lives for their friends. You are my friends if you obey me. *John 15:13-14, NLT*

But the problem is we've all sinned against God (Romans 3:23)— we want to do everything our own way. We deserve punishment, and yet Christ took it for us. What's our part? We need to make some choices: Believe that Christ died for us; tell him we're sorry for our sin, and that we want to be changed; and invite Jesus to be our Forever-Friend and Savior for the rest of our lives. And then we will have the best unconditional friend and life transformer anyone could ever have!

True-Blue

Accepting Jesus as your friend and Savior, guard and guide is the only condition to having him as the #1 true-blue Friend who'll never leave you.

Have you accepted Christ into your heart as Savior, friend, guard, and guide? If not, why not?

_____

_____

If you have accepted Christ previously, has he become your friend? How? Is your relationship with him exciting and constantly growing?

_____

_____

Christ longs for a close relationship with you. His one condition is that you accept him whole-heartedly as your #1 priority. Ask God to help make you willing to discover more about him. Make these verses your prayer:

> I pray also that the eyes of your heart may be enlightened in order that you may know the hope to which he has called you, the riches of his glorious inheritance in the saints, and his incomparably great power for us who believe. _Ephesians 1:18-19_

DAY FIVE
The Forever Friend

Brandon's heart ached. He couldn't believe it could hurt so much—even after five years.

Last weekend he'd been invited to a barbecue with his friend Chaka's family. He had watched them all work together to get lunch ready—they were having so much fun. Brandon wished he had a dad. But his dad had left when Brandon was ten, and he could hardly even remember what his dad looked like. His mom had put away all the pictures in a locked drawer.

Just once, God! his soul cried. *Why can't I have a dad like that— just for one day!* Oddly enough, that Wednesday, his youth group leader talked about how God is not only our Father—which Brandon had a hard time with because he thought fathers were bogus— but our Best Friend. And even better, a forever friend who is always with us wherever we go.

Brandon hadn't prayed for a long time. Up till now, he really hadn't felt God cared much about him, or God wouldn't have let his dad leave. But tonight, he prayed, "God, please be my dad. And, God, be my forever friend too. I really need one. Amen." He felt happy for the first time in months.

Best Friends

If you've accepted Christ into your heart and life, you're his child. It's pretty wonderful to have a Best Friend and Daddy all wrapped up in one. God is proud to call us his own: "For none of us lives to himself alone and none dies to himself alone. If we live, we live to the Lord; and if we die, we die to the Lord. So, whether we live or die, we belong to the Lord" (Romans 14:7-8).

The Power in You

When Jesus left earth and ascended to heaven, he didn't leave us alone to fend for ourselves. He sent the Holy Spirit to help us every day (John 14:16-17). And he gives us a huge promise:

> "So do not fear, for I am with you;
> do not be dismayed for I am your God.
> I will strengthen you and help you;
> I will uphold you with my righteous right hand."
> *Isaiah 41:10*

The Best Is Yet to Come

God promises the best is yet to come. Earth's like living in a garbage can compared to what's in heaven! And God's preparing a place for you. Just think—your very own room in the grandest mansion of all. But the best thing is that you'll be with your Favorite Friend in a place where no tears will fall. Ever. That's *got* to be a fairy-tale ending.

Jesus wants to be your Forever Friend. How can you draw closer to him this week?

_____

_____

Jesus is coming back at a time no one expects. What do you need to do to get your heart and mind ready to go with him?

_____

_____

Thank God today for the promises of his Word. Ask him to remind you constantly of his love and friendship for you.